INTRODUCING MEISTER ECKHART

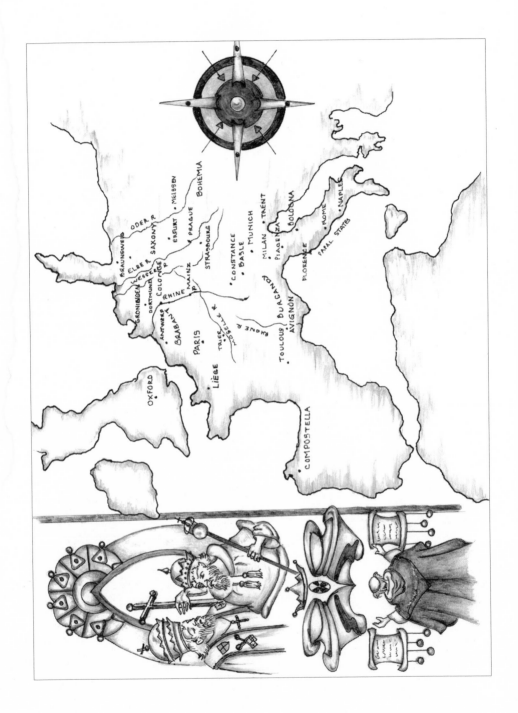

Introducing
Meister Eckhart

Michael Demkovich OP

Illustrations by Robert Staes OP
Foreword by Timothy Radcliffe OP

Liguori/Triumph

LIGUORI, MISSOURI

Imprimi Potest:
Thomas D. Picton, C.Ss.R.
Provincial, Denver Province
The Redemptorists

Published by Liguori/Triumph
An imprint of Liguori Publications
Liguori, Missouri
www.liguori.org

Originally published under the same title by Novalis, Saint Paul University, Ottawa, Canada, 2005.

Library of Congress Catalog Card Number: 2006929047
ISBN-13: 978-0-7648-1507-2
ISBN-10: 0-7648-1507-5

Liguori Publications, a nonprofit corporation, is an apostolate of the Redemptorists. To learn more about the Redemptorists, visit Redemptorists.com.

Printed in the United States of America
10 09 08 07 06   5 4 3 2 1

First U.S. Edition

For my parents,
Joe and Jean Demkovich

Contents

Acknowledgements

As a novice I first met Meister Eckhart in a small, dusty novitiate library where Blakney's translation waited for me to to discover it. In the mid 1970s, very little was available in English on Eckhart, so to whichever friar left that book and paved the way for my first encounter with this amazing mystic, I am grateful. The novitiate was a time of deep personal prayer for me, and Eckhart became a welcome guide. Later, when I was sent to Belgium for doctoral studies, I returned once more to Eckhart: not for prayer this time, but for study.

Meister Eckhart is a Dominican who makes sense in a Dominican context. This is a context that many people do not understand or know, but one that must be acknowledged as significantly formative of Eckhart. Being a Dominican says so much about the individual: common aspects to Dominican life shape a person to see the world in a particular way. For a person who is formed in this way of life, it becomes part of their spiritual DNA. We can readily identify most people from the way they are; people from different regions are socialized, formed by their environment. So, too, with religious community: a person is socialized, formed by a particular environment, a way of life, called a charism. It is sometimes difficult for people to understand that religious communities, even today, hand on a particular way of life. For Dominicans, this way of life is a love for study and prayer that is ordered to preaching. Handed on over time, it conveys a world of meaning that I feel I share with Eckhart.

In writing a book like this, the process I undertook echoes the creative force at work in Eckhart and the Creator at work in our world. I want to thank my parents, family and friends who supported me through this process. I am grateful to a number of people along the way who read the manuscript in its various forms, and politely encouraged me. I am especially indebted to numerous conversations with students, retreatants and colleagues, and the constructive insights and support offered by Simon Gaine, OP, Joan See and Kelly-Jo Kuchar. I want to extend a special word of thanks to Robert Staes, OP, and to Novalis for their willingness to take on this project. Finally, I want to thank Timothy Radcliffe, OP, for finding the time to write the foreword, Kevin Burns for his guidance, Anne Louise Mahoney and the editorial staff at Novalis for their incredible patience.

In the midst of active ministry, I am grateful to the Province of St. Albert the Great for giving me the time to devote to Eckhart. I owe a special thanks to the English Province of Dominicans at Blackfriars, Oxford, for their hospitality and the use of their library, which was extremely valuable. Eckhart is an amazing spiritual guide and mentor whom I hope you, too, will meet as guide and mentor in the pages of this book.

Michael Demkovich OP
September 2005

Foreword

Meister Eckhart was a German Dominican born around 1260. In his time, he was famous as a theologian and a mystic. Then, for centuries, he was largely forgotten. Now he is a spiritual teacher who is appreciated by Christians, Buddhists, and other believers, by scholars and people who just wish to draw nearer to God, or discover the God who is already at the centre of our lives. Eckhart is a figure of the Middle Ages who can be difficult to understand, and yet his images are often so startling that they reach across the centuries and grab our hearts and minds. Michael Demkovich OP offers here a short introduction to Eckhart's thought that helps us to find our way to its vital centre.

If we think of mystics and spiritual teachers, we probably imagine them locked in solitude and silence, wrapped up in God, abstracted from the world, transcending rational reasonable thought. None of this is true of Eckhart. He was deeply involved in the issues of his day and thought penetratingly, even if sometimes paradoxically.

Eckhart was loved and trusted by his brethren who elected him to be Provincial of his Province of Saxony, among other offices. He was also elected to be Provincial of the new Province of Teutonia, but the Order had other plans. A practical man, he knew the art of government, and got on well with women and men. He spent much of his life travelling around his Province, and indeed Europe, on foot or on a donkey. He understood how ordinary people lived and knew how to touch their minds and imaginations. For him, the spiritual life was not an ethereal existence that leaves us floating six feet above the ground; he rejected any dualism of mind and body. Rather, for him, the spiritual life was grounded on the soil of our everyday existence, as we struggle with ordinary, everyday decisions. His spirituality is made for people who are immersed in the world and its complexity.

At the centre of his teaching is what is usually called "detachment," though Demkovich argues that "unattachment" is a better term. This is not a rejection of the world. Instead, it is that unpossessiveness of things that makes us light-hearted and free for the pilgrimage to God. For those medieval friars it was obviously linked with the vow of poverty, but it was more than that. It was part of the liberty of every Christian.

Eckhart would also have rejected any dichotomy between spirituality and hard thinking. He was a theologian who was appointed to be a Master in the University of Paris, the greatest centre of intellectual life in medieval Europe. There he learned the art of teaching clearly, if provocatively. Reason is not for him cerebral faculty, coldly dissecting the world. It is, as Demkovich points out, "relational." It opens us up to other people. It helps us draw near to God. Like St. Thomas Aquinas, Eckhart's own Master, Eckhart believed that understanding made one like that which one understood. Stretching our mind open to the mystery of God transforms who we are.

Because Eckhart is both attractive and difficult, it is important to choose the right way into his thought. He is, as Demkovich beautifully puts it, a mug with many handles. Demkovich chooses Eckhart's understanding of the soul as the thread that can guide us to the centre of his teaching. "Soul" is not a part of many people's vocabulary today. Demkovich rises valiantly to the challenge of exploring what this word meant for Eckhart, and what it can mean for us. It may seem a mysterious substance that waits for release from the prison of the body, but Eckhart was convinced of the profound unity of human life: of the soul, the mind and the body. We are deeply one. The soul is "the truest reality of being human"; it is the ground of our life, from which we flourish or wither. It is also where we are one with God, who brings us into being in every moment, and gives birth to the Son in us. We are shown how the spiritual life is deeply linked with our physical life. Eckhart even speaks of the Trinity in terms that are rooted in our very physicality, with the Father resounding in our guts, the Son in our heads and the Spirit in our hearts.

To help us climb the stairway of Eckhart's thought, Demkovich gives us two aids. First, he quotes many of Eckhart's *exampla*, the examples he gives that so wonderfully catch our imagination. I have two favourites. The first describes how we need some still point in this turbulent life: we are like people drifting down a river who, when they wish to sleep, put down the anchor so that they may be still. The second compares the person who is searching for Christ to the hound that has caught the scent of a rabbit. If the hound gets ahead of or beside the rabbit, he loses the scent. The beautiful illustrations by Bob Staes OP help us find the scent of Eckhart's own thought and keep our enthusiasm alive.

We are not sure of Eckhart's Christian name, though he was probably called John. He was known everywhere as "Meister," the Master. He was a spiritual Master and a theological Master. He was a Master of life, who understood the struggles of ordinary people. It is strange that this Master faced such difficult final years, when he was attacked for his views and accused of heresy. He appealed to the pope in Avignon, and went there for trial. Some propositions were extracted from his writings and condemned as heretical, though he himself was not condemned. Why did this happen? Demkovich shows that Eckhart and the Dominican Order were probably caught up in the political conflicts of the time and, to some extent, were pawns in the power games of the empire and the papacy. It is also true that the paradoxical and startlingly way in which he expressed himself meant that it was easy to misunderstand what he wrote and think that he was making very curious assertions indeed! Now he is recognized universally as a Master for us all, of any faith or no faith. We may not know where he is buried, but he continues to bear fruit now and for the future.

Timothy Radcliffe OP

Introduction

To most people, attempting to read Meister Eckhart (1260–1327) seems a very challenging task, like taking in all of the Grand Canyon in one visit. His ideas are marvellous to see but at the same time they seem bigger than we can fully comprehend. The ideas found in his writings and sermons are difficult even if one is a trained theologian, and his language can be confusing. And yet, even given these challenges, the average reader is drawn to the well of wisdom given to this man "from whom God hid nothing," as his student Johannes Tauler described him.

Today, widespread interest in the mystics, and in Meister Eckhart in particular, suggests that modern society senses its lack of holy mystery. Such gaps or voids in our world, like the Grand Canyon, fascinate us. In the last century, studies on Eckhart flourished, which indicates his appeal to the gaping questions and issues of our own age. How can we let go and be less attached to things? What is at the core of who I am? How can I break through the barriers of life? These are just a few of the questions we face.

What is so appealing about this medieval mystic? How could the writings of an almost forgotten fourteenth-century friar preacher capture the minds and hearts of so many different kinds of people and groups, from New Agers to traditionalists, from deconstructionists to universalists, from devout churchgoers to disenfranchised individualists. To answer these questions we must study Eckhart's life, his times, his ethos, and the various influences at play in the drama of his life. After all, mystics were men and women of their times. If they are to speak in our times, we must first hear them in their own.

Meister (or Master) Eckhart catches the interest of most people who read him because he has the ability to integrate life and understanding, sweetly blending the temporal and the eternal. He is able to do this because of his respect for the truth of things. In Eckhart's sense of the eternal, the realities of this life are not lost. When he was called upon to defend his orthodoxy before the tribunal at Cologne, he chose to hold up the whole of his life and teaching as testimony. In doing so, he suggests a moral dimension to his mystical understanding of the Truth that can be seen in the reality of his life. Mysticism for Eckhart was about who a person is, seen in how he or she lives life – the moral dimensions of life. In commenting on John 1:4, he explains this moral dimension of one's life: "'Life was the light of humankind,' morally this wants to say that this life edifies and illumines our neighbour more perfectly than do words."[1] This Master sought integrity of mind and heart, sincerity in words and deeds, which would build up one's neighbour and one's self. Rather than pursuing a "me first" mentality, we are here to help one another find the true self, which is bigger than the ego. It is the soul of who we are!

This distinctively human aspect of what makes us who we truly are is captured in the medieval understanding of the soul. Soul was not seen as just the intellect, memory and will, but was experienced as sparkling with something of the divine, something Godly in the individual human person because we are designed by God to know ultimate perfection. True knowledge is not about knowing a number of categories, such as Aristotelian or Platonic world views. True knowledge is something that transforms us. This is a lesson Eckhart no doubt learned from his Dominican brother Thomas Aquinas on the virtues. In Eckhart's day the Dominicans, following Aquinas's lead, were the edgier thinkers, upsetting the status quo. For them, knowing the Truth was key. When we really know something, it changes us. Ideas help us discover our ideal self, while the lack of them literally leaves us idiots, alone with the *id*. Consequently, it is not enough to "read" Eckhart the way we read a novel. We need time to ponder his thoughts in order to rediscover that life itself is the transforming part of mysticism. Eckhart wisely held that "understanding is a sort of conformity to God,"[2] which he called *deiformity* (God-formity). When we rightly understand our world, we are drawn into or formed into the mystery of God. The integrity of this transformative understanding holds appeal for our postmodern world, a world that questions scientific reason for its lack of moral integrity.

Eckhart explains "transformative knowing" in his comments on the Book of Genesis. God, whose knowledge and action are one, brings forth all created things by divine *fiat*.

This knowing far surpasses how we humans know and act in our world. He tells us:

> Our actions and derived knowledge spring from things and therefore depend on things, changing as things change. Conversely, a thing itself has its origin in divine knowledge and depends on it so that even though things change, since they come after, God does not change.[3]

In a certain sense, we know because reality helps us to know. God has packed the world with these lessons, and the more we learn the lessons, the more we are changed. Our sense of things changes with changes in our comprehension of the things we know. A truly adult understanding is one that has grown along the way. This is not the case with God. God's knowing causes all created things to be. God does not learn from things the way we do. Rather, God teaches us through creation, if we study the world God made. Knowledge, for Eckhart, is not detached impersonal scientific knowledge, a bunch of facts to be manipulated. Human knowledge stands in proper relation with its Godly origin, which teaches us about life. This means that there is a moral relation to our knowing. This helps explain the kind of shift in thinking demanded of the modern reader who wishes to understand Eckhart and his sense of true knowledge. Today, our notion of knowledge has been reduced to the level of ideology. "Spin" has replaced genuine knowledge. What you can get other people to think of as true must be true. Long hidden in the shadows of history, Eckhart has re-emerged with a seemingly new approach to human understanding. It is what I call relational reason,[4] or a kind of moral reason that transforms us into God. What we know does change who we are! This is why Truth was so important to Eckhart. True knowing brings about true change. Being honest about who you are is the surest way to be who you are.

In our attempt to study Meister Eckhart, we know him according to the things known to us, filtered through time and our experiences. That is why scholarship over the past decades has had a major impact on how we now understand not only Eckhart, but what we know about medieval life, or how we appreciate the religious longings of the people to whom Eckhart ministered. What we now know about Eckhart has changed as time has stripped away the misrepresentations of his thought and allowed us to glimpse more clearly his sense of relational knowing. As students of Eckhart, we attempt to approach the unfiltered facts of this man. These facts have many facets. Some come from his own writings, some from writings about him, others from the context of his times, and still others from the overall integrity of his life. We cannot fully understand the Meister from just his writings, what he called *scientia* in Latin and "book learning" (*buchlehren*) in German. To really meet Eckhart we must also learn from his life, what he called "life learning" (*lebenslehren*). We have all met authors or teachers whom we first knew from their writings or lectures, only to be disappointed when we see how they live. Knowing how someone lives is important in having a sense of the person. The texts are not enough; we seek another level of knowledge. Here, science surrenders to *ethos*, a feel for what is right about the person. This means that in learning about Eckhart we must try to know him rightly, in word and deed, if we want to learn the Truth God discloses in his life.

Common Mistakes

So, how does one communicate to an audience or to readers these complex realities and difficult ideas found in Meister Eckhart? It is the rare person who picks up the medieval German text and easily begins reading this mystic. Most of us have met Eckhart through other works. Many English readers have met him through the writings of Oliver Davies, Matthew Fox, Richard Woods or Bernard McGinn.

In the 1980s, references to Eckhart popped up in works on Buddhism, feminism, deconstructionalism (both literary and philosophical) and New Age movements. The technical word for how we meet a historical work, especially a text that has been handed on over centuries, is its "reception." Our modern reception of Eckhart is filtered through various lenses created centuries ago. Unfortunately, this reception has given us a mixed bag of readings or interpretations, including outright falsehoods about Eckhart. A perfect illustration of what I mean can be seen in the historical preservation of an old, run-down house that we want to restore. Walls may have been moved, rooms completely altered, additions made, but we want to do our best to put it back the way it was. We might not find all the original pieces, but we do our best to fill in the gaps as best we can, given what we know. For the same reason, we need to discard the bits that are not true to the house. Just as we might determine to tear up the shag carpet put down in the 1970s, or strip away layers of paint, or try to match the original wallpaper, we must make informed choices in our study of Eckhart. A well-restored home allows us to understand something about the people who used to live there. The integrity of our choices will likewise have an impact on how we "restore" Eckhart.

For the beginner, ignorance of these receptions can make things very confusing. In fact, I have found that what people need most is a correction of the false impressions and misinformation they have about Eckhart. Perhaps the most widespread error is the belief that Meister Eckhart was a heretic. This is absolutely false! It is true that he was tried for heresy, and that a number of propositions alleged to be his were condemned, but he himself (like Thomas Aquinas) was never condemned. In fact, Pope John XXII (1316–1334) went out of his way to state that Eckhart died a faithful son of the Church. Eckhart himself rejected the condemned propositions and any of his own teachings, as he said, "in so far as they could cause heresy."

However, some of his heretical-sounding propositions, it was agreed, were open to very orthodox interpretations.

The second common error is the idea that Eckhart was a radical anti-institutionalist who promoted a gospel of self-actualization without the structures of religion. This error has its root in nineteenth-century German Romanticism, which interpreted Eckhart through the lens of "nature mysticism." This movement, which promoted a German primal spirit, saw in Eckhart a precursor. It is true that Eckhart was one of the first theologians to break out of the formal Scholastic Latin of his time and creatively use the German language. He even made up German words to capture the theological nuances. But his actions were wrongly seen by later generations as a rejection of the Latin ecclesiastical order in favour of a more primitive, folksy way of doing theology. Because of this approach, they portrayed him as one of the early sources of a nationalistic awakening for the Fatherland. They made Eckhart their poster child, fitting him to their agenda. Even the Nazis put Eckhart to their use in promoting the notion of a superior race, holding him up as an independent German, breaking away from Scholastic Latin to create German words for theology.[5]

The third common error about Eckhart, and about Christian mysticism in general, is the equation of Christian mysticism with Gnostic and occult forms of mysticism. While all mysticism shares neo-Platonic roots, Christian mysticism has always enjoyed the corrective of the Incarnation. Rather than fleeing the world and living on an extraterrestrial plane, Christian mystics have preserved a social and moral dimension that remains centred in the life of Christ. As you will see, Eckhart was no escapist. If anything, he was a practical person, very much aware of the ethical demands and moral obligations of the Christian life. If the reader assumes that all mysticism is the same, he or she will miss the unique contribution of Christian mysticism and of Eckhart's mysticism in particular.

Further Challenges

Most readers face another kind of problem in tackling Eckhart's ideas. They often find Eckhart difficult to read because of his familiarity with and easy use of many philosophical concepts that are now foreign to most of us. How do we talk about something like the spiritual realm? Most of us are ill-equipped for such a task. If we do attempt to speak about the spiritual, we soon discover that our categories, our vocabulary and our concepts are inadequate. Few of us have studied the kind of language needed to discuss things that are beyond the physical realm. Yet Eckhart has the categories and concepts we lack, and is very much at home with a religious vocabulary, even fabricating new words to name these ideas. The language Eckhart used is called Metaphysics. Here is where any beginner encounters the greatest difficulties. By not knowing Metaphysics, we limit Eckhart to a very subjective level, misunderstanding the terms he uses. This is more common than you may think. When someone speaks to us in a foreign language, we listen for words that sound familiar to us. We may assume that these familiar words mean what they mean to us; we reduce the meaning to our level. This can be a dangerous practice, however: if you do this in Germany and someone offers you something that sounds like "gift," you might end up dead, since the word in German means "poison." Likewise, if we assume that Eckhart is only talking about our own ego, about our own level of experience, about what it means to us, we cannot grasp his meaning. For Eckhart, concepts such as "humanity" and "nature" are not just about us; they hold profound philosophical meaning. This is especially true of that most difficult concept called the human soul. Sadly, this is a concept foreign to most modern readers. In his summary of Eckhart's preaching, Alois M. Haas identified four essential elements in Eckhart's teachings on the spiritual life: detachment, conformity to God, the nobility of the soul, and the purity of divine nature.[6] All four are incredibly challenging metaphysical concepts that pertain to the soul. This is why it is extremely important for any modern reader of Meister Eckhart to start by appreciating his understanding of the soul, which is more than "I." This idea is addressed in Part II, but be forewarned, understanding it is easier said than done.

While Eckhart presents challenges to today's reader, many people in Eckhart's own day probably did not really understand what he was trying to say either. Some of them thought the same way they lived, as merchants and artisans, trading and crafting things. This "thingly thinking" would find Eckhart's "no-thing" concepts difficult. Concepts like "God-beyond-God," or his prayer that God rid him of God, would not fit into their more materialistic categories. Eckhart himself referred to such people as "coarse-minded." Their concepts and categories of thought did not allow the finer grains of truth to enter their minds. Others, however, grasped these ideas of Eckhart, who we know was a masterful preacher. They so liked his message that they even took notes of his German sermons. For this reason, fortunately, we have copies of many of his sermons, even though there are few autographs of Eckhart's German works. (At that time, 300 years before Gutenberg's printing press, an *amanuensis* or note-taker would have served as recorder, and a limited number of handwritten copies would be made available.)

Word Pictures

How was it that this great university scholar was able to capture the minds of so many people? The answer, I believe, is found in his use of illustrations, word pictures that stay in our minds and help to explain difficult ideas. Most of us are familiar with the legend of St. Patrick holding up a shamrock to explain the concept of the Trinity, how God is both three and one; the parables of Jesus are a similar kind of illustration. These types of illustrations are common to Eckhart. The use of such anecdotes can be traced back to Gregory the Great

(d. 604). Furthermore, another Dominican (like Eckhart) who had been Master of the Order, Humbert of Romans (d. 1277), wrote a treatise "On the Formation of Preachers." He advised the use of such *exempla* or anecdotes to help people less capable of understanding to catch the preacher's point, entertain the crowd and draw an audience.[7] Today we know how powerful graphic images can be, while acknowledging that the imagination is still stronger. For example, we lament Hollywood's rendition of our favourite book, when the movie falls short of how we saw the story in our mind. The imagination is a remarkable tool when used for learning.

In teaching, I have found that often these illustrations most help the beginner appreciate the ideas found in Eckhart. I was first aware of this when I gave a retreat on Meister Eckhart in Albuquerque, New Mexico, using my own stick drawings. Somehow, even with my limited renditions, people could catch on to what were in fact complicated ideas in Meister Eckhart. I began exploring this approach in other retreats, talks and conferences on Eckhart and had the same results. The idea for an illustrated book on Eckhart was born from these experiences. Artist Robert Staes OP captures, in a style reminiscent of classical illustrations, a sense of the medieval world that was Eckhart's, but in a way that invites us to stay a while in that world. His illustrations reflect various statues, manuscripts and paintings from fourteenth-century Europe that he used for inspiration.

Imagination is an important tool for understanding, as Eckhart's vivid images demonstrate, but people new to Eckhart want a solid, clear account of his life and times, something researched and trustworthy. Part I, therefore, is an accessible introduction to various aspects of Eckhart's life and world. Chapter 1 covers the facts of Eckhart's life, while Chapter 2 offers a glimpse into the spiritual depth of this man as seen in the difficult circumstances at the end of his life.

In Part II, I turn to what I believe is the most crucial concept for people to grasp if they genuinely want to understand Eckhart: his concept of the soul. This fundamental concept of how God made us is key to appreciating Eckhart's mysticism. Whatever is most human and humane about us arises from what is most true in the depth of our being, which for Eckhart is the human soul. It is here that Meister Eckhart's illustrations or *exempla* prove most helpful. Chapter 3 presents the basic concept of the soul, while Chapter 4 examines the life of the soul and God's dwelling in the soul. Understanding the human soul and its role in the project of life is what Eckhart wanted to get across to his listeners, and what the modern reader must also "hear." As a skilled teacher and preacher, he knew how to engage the imagination so that the mind could comprehend, or at least come closer in its comprehension. These *exempla* are vehicles for understanding. They help us glimpse the larger truths of life but are not themselves the final goal. For Eckhart, the soul is all about who we are as human beings and what God calls us to become. That is why this concept is worth our effort if we want to appreciate Eckhart's mysticism.

Finally, in Part III, I present a number of Eckhart's *exempla* for the reader to reflect upon in light of this illustrated introduction. This provides an opportunity for the reader readily to engage the spiritual lessons found in Eckhart without too much discouragement. They are freshly cut blooms of his spirituality, drawing us by their fragrance and beauty towards their insight. However, they are cut from the garden and are not the flowering plant itself. My hope is that by offering you, the reader, these few flowers, I might draw you to a deeper study of Eckhart's mysticism, which requires a certain gardening of the mind if it is to grow.

Throughout the book I have enlisted the help of Fr. Bob Staes, a fellow Dominican and artist, to put on paper the images that Eckhart draws with words. I researched the works and style of art appropriate to this period, the late thirteenth and early fourteenth centuries. (I have included a list of the works that served as models for the renditions used in this book.) The art of Eckhart's times inspired, instructed and inculturated people into a social order. Art offered a compelling means of socialization. The visual image remains a very powerful vehicle even today, of course. Fr. Staes rendered the many copies of statues, maps and manuscripts into a style that lends itself to the mind's imagination. The saying "a picture paints a thousand words" has some truth, but at the same time, the image is just that: an image. How we "read" these images is another aspect of understanding Eckhart's creative genius. It has been a creative and enjoyable process to work with an artist in this way, whose theological text is not written in words but drawn in images. The drawings help us understand Eckhart's ideas but they are only a help. My hope is that you will use the *exempla*, or illustrations, as a springboard for contemplating the larger reality, to meet the profound spiritual insights they contain.

Eckhart's World and Ours

Many of us find it hard to remember the past. We tend to focus on what we like and gloss over what is painful or difficult. History is a lot like our memories. Some things have been preserved and documented, while others are less clear. Like Swiss cheese, what makes history interesting is its holes. What we don't know we assume is unimportant, or assume that it was no different than today. Meister Eckhart lived almost 800 years ago. His world was similar to ours in some ways, but in other ways it was very different. If we want to appreciate Meister Eckhart, we need to take a look at some of these differences.

Most of the West is secular; not because people are all atheists, but because our thinking about the world is usually along physical or scientific lines. We tend not to look for the sacred, or a sense of mystery, in our daily lives. While we bracket out religion or are taught to leave it at home, Eckhart's world was marked by religious realities. The Church – and here we must remember that there was only one Church in Eckhart's day – was interwoven in a person's life. The bells of the various churches and monasteries in towns and in the country marked the hours of the day: the liturgical hours. Days were reckoned for their liturgical significance, such as St. Michael's Day (September 29), the feast of St. Blaise (February 3), and the feast of Joachim and Anne (July 26). Towns held special celebrations on their feast days, the day of their patron saints, such as October 9 in Paris (feast of their patron, St. Denis), or October 10 in Cologne (feast of the martyred Roman soldier St. Gereon). The life of the parish, with its daily Mass and its preaching, would generate some discussion in town, and perhaps some gossip. In one sense, the church, especially in the smaller places, was the only show in town. Shops would close for Mass; towns would swell with visitors to a shrine or other place of pilgrimage. If the town had a renowned preacher or a living saint, a person famous for his or her holiness, people would come just to see and hear the holy one.

Another major difference between our world and Eckhart's is how people shopped and conducted business. Today we are consumers. We are accustomed to shopping at superstores, to looking for bargains and sales. We buy items that have been mass-produced in factories on the other side of the world. In major cities, the basics – milk, butter, eggs, bread, and more – are available 24 hours a day, seven days a week. We are used to the convenience of shopping and expect an item to be stocked and on the shelf when we want it; when it isn't, we are annoyed. This consumerist mentality is so much a part of our lives in the Western world that we often don't realize how it shapes our thinking. We expect to be able to buy just about anything. If it's not here at this store, we will drive across town to get it, or order it online. Distances are not a major concern for us. We are people on the move, no

INTRODUCING MEISTER ECKHART

longer tied to our homes or even our home phones. We are mobile and can be available almost anywhere in the world our calling plan works.

Eckhart's world, by contrast, was mercantile. People didn't use money to buy things; they traded goods that they made: cheese, bread, knives, pots, fabric, tapers, and many other items. These items weren't mass-produced but crafted. The more prominent craftspeople formed guilds, an association of master craftsmen who trained their young apprentices and handed on their skills. Eckhart's world did not know the concept of quick convenience. Things took time and life was much more basic: water was fetched, toilets consisted of chamber pots that had to be emptied, food was cooked on open fires or woodburning stoves. Most people stayed in their own region, not venturing too far from home. Life consisted of a steady routine of regular activities all ordered to the basics of life. Travel might be required by merchants or members of town councils or churchmen, but travel was not comfortable or convenient.

Another significant difference between Eckhart's world and ours is political concerns. We think of ourselves as citizens and tend to be loyal to our home country. In Eckhart's time, loyalty would have been to blood relatives or clans. People were loyal to the land, which had been inherited or farmed and worked for the same landlord for generations. People in Eckhart's time were more tied to their region than their nation. In some ways, people were very provincial; those who came from the outside were either regarded with suspicion or esteemed for the news they brought. Stories about the archbishop or the pope or the duke or the emperor came from such travellers. The notion of personal rights as we know it did not exist, although some people received privileges because of their associations. Pontifical dispensations and imperial decrees could mean privileges given to entire towns, such as a town charter, or to people, such as professors at Paris, or the Dominicans

28

and Franciscans: privileges to appeal to the university or to the pope in cases brought by local magistrates.

Unlike us, people of Eckhart's time did not take for granted the issue of quality of life. Most children in the West today have access to formal education. Our world is driven by what we know, and education is the key to getting ahead. In Eckhart's day, education was not available to everyone; it was tied to specific classes of people, usually the upper classes. Merchants, clerics and nobles were educated; the rest learned from experience or by listening to educated people.

If people had "free time," there wasn't much to do for entertainment. In any case, for most people, being idle was not seen as a good thing. One place a person could sit and be idle, however, was at prayer in church. Recreation time was used for lighter labour, such as mending or sewing, but most of what we would consider free time was spent doing the necessary things for family life: securing the home from the elements, wild creatures and thieves; preparing a fire for the cold nights; bringing out the bedding. For the educated and wealthy, some time was available for music, hunting, devotional reading, pilgrimage or social conversation.

For clerics and their counterparts among the monks and friars, education made them valuable secretaries, envoys and administrators. These clerics were employed by their bishops, abbots, superiors and nobles to conduct state affairs, negotiate marriages or treaties, and so on. For someone like Eckhart, who was a mendicant friar, a fairly new kind of religious order, the days were ruled by a pattern of prayer, study, preaching and religious life. The mendicant orders had been established a century earlier by the Church to provide a more mobile or itinerant form of religious life. Most famous of these orders are the Dominicans and Franciscans; Eckhart was a Dominican. These friars, as they were called, could be moved across territories and countries, from one house to another, creating a kind of web of information and resources. This web was held together by a keen sense of obedience; for Dominicans, it was a life vowed in obedience.

This idea of lifelong commitment is strange to many people today, and even a bit scary. To appreciate Eckhart's world we need to realize the significance of religious commitment, of a pledge or sacred oath. People commonly entered into solemn agreement with one another – a king or bishop with their people, a couple with each other and with God in marriage, or a priest or religious with God in religious vows. The sacredness of such vows was binding; violating it had serious consequences. Obedience was mandatory, and a solemn pledge made one accountable before God. Obedience to the authorities in one's life ensured the smooth running of the institution, the effective impact of an organization, and achievement of the institutional goals. Disloyalty, betrayal, duplicity and abuse of power were all serious infractions against this world order. A Dominican was loyal to his Order. Eckhart was first and foremost a Dominican, a preacher and teacher.

In the following chapters I wish to introduce you to Meister Eckhart, his life and times, his understanding of the soul and his spiritual insights. Like all such introductions, this one is but the start of a potential relationship. As you come to know him and his spirituality, may you meet a good friend. And may Eckhart, in turn, introduce you to the God beyond God.

A Note About the Illustrations

Fr. Bob Staes's engaging illustrations were born of a collaborative effort and are inspired by various works of art from Eckhart's time. The medieval artists captured more than just an image; they provide a "snapshot" into the fashion, style and culture of their times. In my research a variety of medieval artifacts kept surfacing; I shared them with Bob, along with my manuscript and a list of about thirty desired illustrations. That was the start of the illustrations found in this book.

In this note I would like to share some of the original pieces that inspire Bob's rich illustrations.

While we don't have newsreels or videos to give us a glimpse into Eckhart's times, happily we do have a variety of artistic sources. We have works that were clearly religious, depicting Old and New Testament scenes, but we have more. The thirteenth century was a time when nobles, knights and benefactors were immortalized in stone. These figures capture the clothing, carriage and characteristics of their time for generations that followed. The artists of the times have also left us glimpses into their day, "doodled," in a sense, on the pages of their books. Even great religious works give us a look into the people's mundane concerns.

Many works include what are known as "ornamentations," fancy geometric patterns and floral designs that appeared not only in their books but on ceilings and in stained-glass windows. These give us a feel for the people's sense of balance and beauty. In addition to the ornamentations, medieval maps give us some insight into people's sense of place. But most of all, their great buildings, their churches and town halls, which stand to this day, tell us about the people's sense of space and scale before God. All of these are references not easily footnoted, but just as helpful as a text from the times.

Bob Staes creatively employed these artifacts in his beautiful renditions of Eckhart's world. They are key aspects in our effort to understand Eckhart, to imagine his spiritual insight through the help of images. Let me draw to your attention a few of these.

Bob's image of Eckhart himself deserves special note. An unknown artist simply called "The Master of Naumburg" filled the Cathedral of Naumburg with a treasury of statues depicting various women and men, including Hermann and Reglindis or Timo von Kistritz, people who lived in this German town between Halle and Erfurt on the Salle River a generation before Meister Eckhart.[8] Naumburg has an interesting history and a fascinating story of its foundation in 1000 by a noble who was one of the pretenders to the German throne after Emperor Otto died without an heir. The Margrave of Meissen (margraves were German noblemen ranking above a count) relocated his ancestral home from Jena, building his "new castle" (Neue Burg) on the Salle River. That Margrave was Ekkehart I; a stone figure of his heir Count Ekkehart (also spelled Eckhart), with his wife, Uta, stands in the Naumburg Cathedral. Bob used features from these statues in his drawing of Eckhart.

While no historical evidence can be found to connect Meister Eckhart with the Count Eckhart, the suggestion is appealing when looking for an artistic inspiration. I feel comfortable with this thin connection for several reasons. Naumburg lies in Thuringia, the same region from which Eckhart is thought to have come. He was likely born in one of several towns in the region called Hochheim. One such town is a suburb of Erfurt. Eckhart very likely made his novitiate in Erfurt, which lies less than 60 miles from Naumburg. We know that he was the prior, or superior, there from 1294 to 1300 before being sent to Paris. While such associations do not prove kinship, they can inspire our imagination.

The illustrations in chapters 1 and 2 owe a great deal to the scenes of daily life depicted in the cathedrals and manuscripts of the time. Additional statues from the Naumburg Cathedral, such as those of Mary, the Crucifixion, Christ before Pilate, and Peter's renunciation, give a sense of Eckhart's world. Recall that he was born around 1260, and the Master of Naumburg flourished in the mid-1200s. These and similar works would have been part of Eckhart's youth. Other cathedrals also depict the nobles of the day: the Cathedral of Meissen with its "Benefactors" and the Cathedral of Bamberg with the impressive "Bamberg Rider" (horse and all), along with various chapels and monasteries, are added sources of inspiration. The trimmings, windows, soffits and friezes adorning these buildings all capture the sense of the time, and are reflected in Bob Staes's works.

The use of artistic illustration was common in medieval manuscipts,[9] such as the "Book of the Hours." Biblical and liturgical manuscripts were known by the noble women and men of Eckhart's day and to the religious monks and nuns who relied on large illuminated texts for their prayer. But such illustrations were not limited to religious themes. Both monastic and university libraries had philosophical works with drawings meant to help explain the text. The Ghent "Tree of Good" (*arbor bona*) and "Tree of Evil" (*arbor mala*) are twelfth-century examples, and earlier examples include Empedocles's "Four Elements and Qualities," or Aristotle's "Universe."

A popular theme was that of the vices and virtues. The eleventh-century Klimax manuscript depicting the "Ladder of Virtues," the Bamberg depiction of "Virtues Triumphant," or the twelfth-century Ratisbon manuscript personifying the vices and virtues offer us biblical images of the day. In the thirteenth century, an interesting convention was the connection of the virtues to Christ's Passion. The famous fourteenth-century illustration found in a work by Henry Suso, one of Eckhart's disciples, contains figures of nuns, angels, the devil, death, concentric circles, a line coursing the path and explanatory text as representing the "Mystical Way." Part II, chapters 3 and 4, of this book provide similar illustrations of Eckhart's understanding on the soul. The inner spiritual life and the outer moral life are seen in the drawings inspired by the works just mentioned.

Chapter 5 contains drawings known as "versals" or "Lombardic Capitals" which set off the section and are fanciful embellishments of the first letter in a section, called the uncial. Here Bob Staes creatively and playfully depicts the theme treated in the section. These versals are his interpretation and deserve extra attention. As you read the section, go back to the versal and enjoy Bob's graphic summary.

Eckhart's words are a kind of verbal cartoon. They are words without why, without mediation, naming a reality we can only hold on to by letting go. The mix of graphic images and Eckhart's mystical spirituality are a delightful marriage of abstract theology and creative cartoons. We are familiar with political cartoons that criticize government policy, mock an opponent or capture a cultural moment. These cartoons have a powerful impact. Bob Staes's illustrations have a similar power, touching a depth dimension of the human soul. They explain without explanations and reveal hidden truths long before the word is in our mind.

PART I

The Person

"Who are you?" This question haunts us all; answering it may be a lifelong task.

Who was Meister Eckhart? It has often been said that he was not only a master of the text (*lesemeister*), or scholar, he was also a master of the spiritual life (*lebemeister*). This twofold mastery says a lot about Eckhart. To know him requires a twofold sense. A Dominican named Johannes Tauler, one of Eckhart's disciples, chided people for not understanding his spiritual master. Tauler says: "That was the teaching and these were the words of a most lovable master, but you did not comprehend. For he spoke about eternity, and you understood it in temporal terms."[1] Tauler's words suggest something about Eckhart's twofold personality. Eckhart was "a most lovable master" and a theologian who "spoke about eternity," a master of life and learning. In the next few chapters I would like to introduce you to both the person and the unique spiritual theologian who was Meister Eckhart.

In coming to know Eckhart over my years of research, I have encountered a lot of facts about him. At the same time, many questions remained unanswered: Did he have any brothers and sisters? What made him laugh? How did he die? While we cannot know everything about him, learning about his world, his ideas and his situation help us get a feel for him.

For me there are three important facts about Eckhart. First, he was a Dominican living in a period when the Order flourished. Second, he was brought to trial for suspected heresy and was later exonerated. Third, he was a renowned preacher and teacher. Our knowledge of Eckhart can be grouped around these facts, but our feel for him is found in the details that give richness to these facts. Introducing someone to a friend requires giving enough information for the new acquaintances to engage one another and discover more about each other. In this section, allow me to introduce you to someone I consider a friend and guide. I hope you will come to know him better and will eventually consider him a friend and guide, too. After all, that is the point of introducing Meister Eckhart.

1

I Brother Eckhart:
My Life and Teachings Testify²

Medieval Life of a Friar Preacher

ambulavit dominicus

When we think about it, it is amazing that we can
say much at all about the man Eckhart, whose
life was nearly erased from the pages of history.
What information we have comes to us from his life in the
Dominican Order. This life can be reconstructed from the

program of formation customarily followed in Eckhart's time. In the mid-1900s, the German scholar Josef Koch began to wipe away layers of dust covering Eckhart's story and arrived at what we can consider three historically accurate dates. While some criticize Koch for not establishing more precise dates, I believe his caution is due to the limits of the historical evidence. Better to say honestly no more than the evidence allows.[3] With Koch as our base, we at least have the following dates: "…about 1277 Eckhart was a student of arts in Paris, prior to 1280 he began the study of theology in Cologne, and lectured on [Peter Lombard's Book of] Sentences in Paris, 1293–94."[4] Using these three references, we can roughly put Eckhart's birth at about 1260, with which most scholars agree. However, questions remain about Eckhart's place of birth, his parents and his siblings. Most biographers agree that he was born in one of the two towns called Hochheim in Thuringia. He entered the Dominican novitiate in Erfurt, most likely in 1276, where he learned the Order's way of life.

These were exciting times for the Dominicans; it was a time of new hope. The Council at Lyon in 1274 was to address the centuries-old schism between the East and West. Many prominent theologians were invited to attend; one of them was the Dominican Thomas Aquinas. Tragically, he died on his way to the Council of Lyon, but 20 years later rumours were already circulating about his canonization. He would be canonized in 1323, giving the Dominicans their second saint (St. Dominic had been canonized in 1234). As a novice, Eckhart no doubt heard stories about the great Thomas; we might imagine Eckhart's thoughts about his illustrious predecessors when he himself went to the University of Paris. Paris was an intellectual and international hub, with students from many of Europe's dioceses and religious Orders. (It was not as we think of university today: one had to be a cleric, even if one did not intend to go on to ordination. To this day, some professions have this clerical remnant in the name "clerk.")

That same year, 1277, Humbert of Romans, a former Master of the Dominican Order and author of a popular treatise on preaching, died. During this time, the Dominicans in Paris were challenging the conservative form of Augustinianism. After completing two years of studies, Eckhart returned to Cologne shortly before the death of another famous Dominican, Albert the Great (1280), who had been mentor to Aquinas and a living authority of the day. It is difficult to say if Albert knew Eckhart or held him in the same high regard that Albert had held Aquinas, but there is no doubt that Eckhart fondly recalls Albert, invoking him in his writings. The death of such a great theologian as Albert would have been a profound moment for any 20-year-old Dominican. Perhaps Eckhart was inspired by the greatness of these scholars when he returned to the University of Paris thirteen years later, lecturing on the Sentences of Peter Lombard, as Thomas had done before him.

The end of the thirteenth century was an exciting time for Europe as well. England had achieved representative government under the reign of Edward Longshanks, the first of the Edwards to reform England (1272–1302), establishing the model Parliament in 1295, while the saintly Louis IX had consolidated the French monarchy before his death in 1270, six years before Eckhart entered the novitiate. In Italy, two contemporaries, the poet Dante Alighieri (b. 1265) and the artist Giato di Bondone (b. 1276) were part of the Italian revival that so influenced Europe. Gothic architecture had changed the look of Europe's great edifices. This was the style used at Notre Dame, the cathedral of Paris, and at Erfurt, where Eckhart made his novitiate, the first phase in his Dominican life. With so many developments in politics and culture, Eckhart's world was alive with creative change.

Before Eckhart's fortieth birthday, the brethren of the Erfurt *conventus* (priory) elected him as their Prior, or Superior. This probably took place after his return to Germany from Paris in

1294, when the Order also appointed him provincial vicar of the region of Thuringia. Both of these facts suggest the kind of leadership qualities that we often deny the mystic. Also, it was during these years that he had personal contact with Theodore of Freiburg, the Dominican Provincial of Teutonia, whom Eckhart had replaced as lecturer in Paris when Theodore was elected Provincial (1293–1296).[5] Both men played key roles in shaping what has been called the Rhineland School of mysticism. Eckhart wrote his *Reden der Unterweisung*, or *Counsels on Discernment*, during this period, very likely in 1298. These short "table talks" were brief religious instructions given during the meal to help young Dominicans in their spiritual formation. His term as Prior ended in late 1300, when the Dominican General Chapter of Marseille absolved all conventual Priors of Teutonia from their office.[6] This action may have been due to problems in the Province, but was more likely done in antici-pation of the division of the German Province of Teutonia to create a second province of the northern territory. The latter is the more likely explanation, since two vicars were appointed by the Dominican Master: one friar, Nicholas, was appointed for the north; the other, Hugo, for the south.[7] In 1303, the new Northern Province of Saxony was officially established. Its members elected Eckhart their first leader.

These changes in Teutonia brought changes for many friars, including Eckhart. In 1302, he went to Paris as a teacher at the University, where he held the chair for non-Frenchmen, a position that in the past had been occupied by other Do-minicans such as Albert and Thomas Aquinas. Over the next eleven years, Eckhart would spend two significant though brief stays in Paris teaching at the University. Both stays, 1302–1303 (before he was elected Provincial) and 1311–1313 (after his term) serve as bookends. It was during the in-between years that he served as the first Provincial of the newly established German province of Saxony (1303–1311). These eleven years in Paris and Cologne can truly be called the high points of Eckhart's professional life.

Perhaps a brief explanation of the political reality will help here. Eckhart vowed obedience; he could not pick and choose what he would do or when. Dominican governance was "capitular," which meant that local priories or houses gathered as "chapters" to elect their prior or superior. A province is a federation of priories in a region that in a similar way, "in chapter," elect a provincial. Through a system of checks and balances of rights, priories were independent of one another, but the provincial chapter and the Provincial himself gave direction to the province. Throughout Christendom, these provinces were similar to priories in their independence; the Master of the Order, with his curia or council, enjoyed similar rights over the provinces as Provincials did over priories. This meant that Orders like the Dominicans were multinational corporations that faced geographical and ecclesiastical agendas, both locally and globally.

Relying on the critical research of Joseph Koch as our foundation, we now turn to some additional historical information about Eckhart. First we will examine his years as the new provincial of Saxony. This period provides fascinating stories that allow us to glimpse the practical concerns this mystic faced. We will then turn our attention to Eckhart the scholar and his two terms as Master in Paris. His second stay in Paris was followed by time spent in Strasbourg, where he served as a widely respected spiritual mentor. Finally, we will come to the controversies surrounding his so-called condemnation and the inquisition process. The end of Eckhart's life is as much a puzzle as its start. What would lead a widely respected Master of Paris to face an ecclesiastical tribunal in Cologne and ultimately appeal his case to the Pope in Avignon? The biggest mystery in this puzzle is Eckhart's death.

Introducing a mystic through his accomplishments may seem peculiar. Most people want to jump into the spiritual sayings. I recall one student who complained that I gave too much information on Eckhart's life and times and not enough on his spirituality. I quickly realized that some people want Eckhart to be their own personal guru. But the life of a mystic is far more important than many people will allow. Christian mystics in particular embody a moral dimension in their mysticism. Their life offers us lessons that we need to study if we want to learn their genuine mysticism. I stress Eckhart's life and times because a person's activities tell us something about his or her life, which after all is the inner movement of the person. Spirituality and life are inseparable. Spirituality animates, literally giving life to our beliefs in the here and now. To separate the two is to reduce spirituality to the esoteric and life to the insignificant. Eckhart's life is Eckhart's spirituality.

Provincial of Saxony

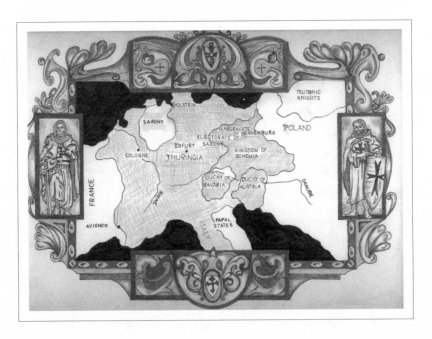

The nine years Eckhart spent as provincial of Saxony (1303–1311) tell the tale of a practical administrator. They tell us something of his personality. Since we lack first-hand accounts of Eckhart's personality, we can catch a glimpse of it in the deeds of his life. Actions do speak louder than words.

We need to remember that Eckhart's time as Provincial was the start of a new venture. It required a person who could lead, govern and negotiate. This new province, it should be noted, included the regions of "Meissen, Thuringia, Hesse, Saxony, Mark Brandenburg, Sclavonia [sic, probably Holstein] (reaching from Hamburg to Stralsund), Friesland, Westphalia, Zeeland and Holland."[8] The territory numbered 47 priories (Dominican monasteries), with three additional houses established by 1310. It was a formidable task for the former prior and professor to undertake in his early 40s. (Later, Eckhart was given additional responsibilities as Vicar for Bohemia.)

The territory that constituted this new province would today cover the northern two-thirds of Germany, the Netherlands and part of the Czech Republic – about the size of Canada's Atlantic provinces or most of New England in the United States. This geography is important for us to bear in mind when we consider that Eckhart's duties as Provincial would require travel, which would have meant simple travel as required by his Order, on foot or by donkey, and rarely (if ever) the luxury of noble travel by horse. Not only would he need to attend to his own territory, but the Dominican Order would also require his participation in their general chapters of all provinces. Interestingly, the Dominican Order remains one of the oldest democratic organizations in existence. It was in these "general chapters" that the business of directing the Order was achieved, while the Master of the Order, elected by a general chapter, served a term and governed the Order.

We know that during Eckhart's term as Provincial there were three general chapters of provincials held during Hemericus of Piacenza's generalate, as well as the other general chapters of provincials and delegates.[9] These chapters of provincials took place in Toulouse (1304), Strasbourg (1307) and Piacenza (1310). We know from the *Acta* of the Dominican Order that Eckhart participated in all three of these chapters.[10] The chapter of Strasbourg named him vicar general for the Bohemian province: there were problems there and the chapter gave Eckhart extensive authority, most likely to reform the province. Reform at any time in history is difficult, but the fact that this task was entrusted to a new provincial of a newly formed province tells us something about Eckhart. This appointment was an indication of the Order's respect for him – for both his loyalty and his orthodoxy. His involvement with the Bohemian reform explains his absence the following year from the chapter of Padua. He was, however, present at Piacenza in 1310, where he gave a full report on his actions in Bohemia. Undoubtedly, he was successful, since the next chapter, held at Saragossa, makes no further mention of the Bohemian problem. Eckhart's role in reforming the Bohemian province deserves note, as some modern readers believe Eckhart to have been opposed to the institutions of his day. Clearly, the Order saw him as a capable and loyal leader. His four years as the new provincial before the 1307 chapter demonstrated that he was a practical, political and competent leader, not a maverick renegade.

Eckhart's involvement was by no means limited to the general chapters of the Order. He also tended to the care and administration of his own young province of Saxony. As we have seen, the great size of this province required of its provincial not only the stamina for travel, but that he be a capable administrator of temporal and spiritual goods as well. Governance within the Dominican Order was, by medieval standards, extremely democratic. Common practice for religious like the Benedictines was an election for life. Dominicans, on the other hand, followed a model whereby the community elected their superior, or leader, for a term.

During his nine years in office, Eckhart held nine provincial chapters, assemblies of priors and elected representatives from his province. It is probable that one additional, earlier chapter, sometime in September of 1303 after the foundation of the new province, took place in Erfurt, where Eckhart had been prior. In any case, beginning in 1304, and every year thereafter on the feast of the Nativity of Mary (September 8) until 1310, provincial chapters were held in the following towns: Halberstadt, Rostock, Halle, Minden, Seehausen, Norden and Hamburg. These chapters indicate the kind of ardour with which Eckhart diligently worked.

In his *Counsels on Discernment*, talks given to the community at Erfurt, Eckhart describes what he understood by this kind of dedication to one's works. For Eckhart, satisfaction is not in the profit, but in the meaningfulness of our work. He tells us:

> A man should never be so satisfied with what he does or accomplish it in such a way that he becomes so independent or overconfident in his works that his reason becomes idle or lulled to sleep. He ought always to lift himself up by the two powers of reason and will, and in this to grasp at what is best of all for him in the highest degree, and outwardly and inwardly to guard prudently against everything that could harm him. So in all he will lack nothing, but he will grow constantly and mightily.[11]

Here we find an early reference to how work and reason serve to integrate the human person. Activity and knowledge, work and reason, seem to be inseparable companions; Eckhart understood this from his first time in office as prior at Erfurt, and especially later as provincial. What we do relates to who we are: this is the basis of a virtuous life. My actions have consequences and they are formative of who I am. Eckhart's work as Provincial, I believe, explains his apparent lack of writings during this time. However, Koch believes that the *Liber Benedictus*, containing *Das Buch der göttlichen Tröstung* (*The*

Book of Divine Consolation), written for the grieving Queen of Hungary on the death of her father, and *Von dem edlen Menschen* (*Of the Nobleman*), which addressed the active life rooted in the core of the spiritual life, can both be dated between 1307 and 1310. This would place them in the midst of his provincialate; they have been considered by some to be the deepest of the Meister's works. These tracts suggest a thinker well aware of human nature in all its sufferings and strivings.

Eckhart enjoyed a favourable reputation among the Dominicans throughout Germany because in 1310, the electors of the neighbouring province, Teutonia, elected him to be their provincial. A Dominican provincial chapter, which is elective, is free to elect anyone in the Order. Afterward, it is the Master of the Order who approves or rejects the election. The general chapter, with a say over the whole Order, could assign a person from one province to a job in another. Of course this did not include elected office such as provincial or prior, but works of the Order, such as teaching. This is what happened in Eckhart's case. Being properly elected by the southern province of Germany, Teutonia, he normally would have been approved. But the general chapter, facing problems at the University of Paris concerning the orthodoxy of Thomas Aquinas, intervened. The General Chapter of Naples (1311) did not approve Eckhart's election and instead reassigned him to Paris.[12]

What is important for us to note is that as both a theologian and an administrator, Eckhart enjoyed the esteem of his Order. Medieval political life often centred on the rights and privileges of the Church, kingdoms, towns, and guilds or other associations, such as the relatively new friars (both the Dominicans and the Franciscans). While force, even today, can remain the final arbiter, most concerns relied on argumentation and law. Eckhart was surprisingly good at this political reality. Before we turn to his teaching career, we need to take a closer look at his talents as a practical mystic-provincial.

Difficulties over Dortmund

In some ways, Eckhart became Provincial at a difficult time. He assumed his new charge amid a somewhat hostile climate: the diocesan clergy were upset with the popular mendicant friars, who were seen as economic and ecclesial threats to the urban diocesan holdings. Yet Eckhart managed to establish three new religious houses or priories even with this opposition. One priory, established in the capital city of

Braunschweig, was designed to house 60 friars and was the largest of the three communities.[13] He founded the second house at Groningen, in present-day the Netherlands. A bit of cleverness got this second house. The knight Ludolph bought it from Lutbert Heddinga and in turn deeded the property to his relative, the Dominican superior or prior of Winsum, Brother Conrad.[14] However, the most intriguing of the three is the third house, founded in Dortmund. Koch says:

> The saga concerning the foundation of the convent in the free imperial city of Dortmund (in the Archdiocese of Cologne) is one of the most turbulent chapters in the history of the German Dominicans.[15]

Of particular significance to the story and to circumstances later in Eckhart's life is that the Archbishop of Cologne, Henry of Virneburg, a Franciscan, had just been consecrated archbishop in 1305, after Eckhart's arrival as provincial. Virneburg was an intense advocate of orthodoxy and church discipline; 20 years later, he would bring Eckhart to trial on charges of false teaching or heterodoxy. One factor in his actions was a growing feud between the Franciscans and Dominicans. The battle over Thomas Aquinas pitted the two orders in the so-called *Correctoria* Controversy, where the Franciscans claimed they were "correcting" Aquinas, eliminating errors they thought present concerning the nature of Christ. The Dominicans quickly called what the Franciscans were doing a "corruption," and controversy ensued. There had long been a sibling rivalry between these two mendicant orders; their vying for recognition and privilege indicates the darker side of ecclesiastical politics. However, the larger political context placed these two orders in opposing camps. As we will see, Europe was beginning to take sides on the question of cross or crown: loyalty to the pope or to the emperor. A closer study of this turbulent period discloses some suspicious events that may have led to Eckhart's subsequent trial and can shed light on this mystic administrator. It is worth studying the circumstances surrounding this Dortmund episode, since it seems to indicate political bad blood with the Franciscan Archbishop of Cologne.

It was after three failed attempts, Koch recounts, that the house in Dortmund was finally established.[16] This was done, however, in opposition to the town council and the clergy of Dortmund. So how did the Dominicans accomplish this feat? Eckhart took advantage of a meeting he had with the Holy Roman Emperor, Henry VII, while both men were in Constance. Eckhart hoped to bring to an end the stalemate that existed over Dortmund. Obviously aware of the Emperor's rights in governing the imperial cities, Eckhart requested on May 26, 1309, approval from the Emperor to erect a priory in the imperial city of Dortmund. Apparently, permission was granted. In July of the same year, a priest sympathetic to the Dominicans, Eberhard of Vrydach (covertly, we may presume), bought property in Dortmund from Gottfried Pallays on behalf of the provincial, Eckhart. They then transferred the land into the hands of the provincial and friars of Saxony. When Eberhard conveyed this fact to the town council, no objections were raised at that time. However, once Eckhart named Friar Gottfried Caput the first prior in 1310 and sent five friars with him to Dortmund, the storm began to brew. By April 2, 1311, one year after the friars arrived, a diocesan priest, Father Arnold St. Reinoldi, along with some other diocesan clergy, had already complained about the Dominicans to the official court at Cologne and won some form of judgment. This legal action prevented the Dominicans from residing in the city. In effect, it expelled them from Dortmund.

We do not know the details of the complaint. However, economic and political tensions between the mendicant orders (who actually lived inside the cities, unlike the older monastic orders, who kept to the country) and the diocesan clergy (who were firmly established in the towns) are well documented. For example, six years earlier, in 1305, Eckhart had to write as provincial to the town council of Göttingen, guaranteeing that the Dominicans there would not increase their urban property without the town council's approval.[17] Perhaps a similar concern prompted Father Arnold St. Reinoldi to bring action against the friars preachers. Regardless of the reason, it was not until May 1330, after Eckhart's death, that the matter was finally resolved. It seems that the Dominicans, due to the energetic support of Pope John XXII, were finally able to remain in Dortmund.[18]

It is more than just suspicion that makes one wonder about this historical gap of 21 years from the Dortmund purchase in 1309 to its legitimate resolution in 1330. The dramatic personalities we see at the end of Eckhart's life ultimately involve Eckhart, the Archbishop of Cologne and the papal court at Avignon. It may be stretching facts a bit, but one can imagine that the Archbishop of Cologne saw Eckhart and the Dominicans as threats to his ecclesiastical rule. As we have seen, Eckhart's years as provincial of Saxony were not without the political realities and consequences of his day. It is also significant to note that the evidence shows some struggle had existed between the Archdiocese of Cologne and the Dominicans during Eckhart's term as provincial. The fact that this struggle is resolved one year after the March 27, 1329, condemnation of Eckhart's theses by Pope John XXII, and (it seems) after Eckhart's death, would suggest something more than mere coincidence was at work behind the curial scene. We will return to this point later.

Eckhart's service to his Order was significant. It remains one solid part of this great man's life, demonstrating his loyalty and respect in the Order. Equally important was his teaching career at the University of Paris, which at that time was a great centre of Christian thought. At Paris, the masters freely employed the writings of the Greek pagan authors, and of Islamic and Jewish philosophers. Eckhart's ability to navigate the spiritual depth of his experience using the theological tools at hand demonstrates his real genius.

Magister in Paris

Eckhart spent two terms teaching at Paris. From his first period as a master teacher, or his *"magisterium"* (1302–1303), we have but a few details. Most new professors of the day would be lecturing and directing students in their work. In addition, they would engage in discussion with the other professors of the university. This was the centre of European intellectual life, an international collection of scholars with different ideas. It was common at Paris for professors to argue with one another. For some, this attracted more students to their roster; for others, it was a way to defend or challenge theories of the day; while for still others, especially among the orders, it was a way to promote an entire approach to the subject. The most noted debates at Paris often involved opposing views on the use of Aristotle. During this time, Eckhart wrote two *Questions*, which argued with the Franciscan Master Gonsalvo. These disputes were arguments over what we today might consider trivial things: for example, over which is more important in the soul, will or intellect; or whether we have one soul or multiple souls. However, on closer examination we see that Eckhart's questions were part of a larger Dominican effort to defend the innovations of the venerable Thomas Aquinas. Aquinas's teachings were being condemned by some at Paris and Oxford. Such disputes were common at Paris, and they reflect the intellectual engagement of that city. Armand A. Maurer indicates that there was an additional disputed question between Eckhart and Gonsalvo during this first Parisian stay.[19] A common disagreement between Dominicans and Franciscans had to do with the powers of the soul and their respective roles. This continued the basic difference between Aquinas and the Franciscan Bonaventure earlier in the thirteenth century. Eckhart argued with Gonsalvo concerning the excellence of the intellect over the will. This point is fundamental to the way Eckhart and the Dominicans thought about the human person. In this life, to know is the greatest gift; the importance of this idea will be discussed in Part II.

As a professor at Paris, Eckhart would also be expected to deliver sermons at the University. These would have been his Latin sermons,[20] which were formal and scholarly in nature. It is difficult to say much more than this about Eckhart's first stay as Master in Paris for the chair for foreigners.

After leaving Paris, Eckhart served as provincial of the newly established province of Saxony. We saw how capably he met the challenges of these years. After this term, which included being elected to the same job in the neighbouring German province of Teutonia, the Order sent Eckhart back to Paris. He must have done an impressive job as provincial of Saxony for the province of Teutonia to elect him to be their Provincial; there must have been some pressing need that would cause the General Chapter to ignore the vote of Teutonia and send Eckhart to Paris.

In his second term at Paris (1311–1313), after Eckhart had been seasoned by nine years as Provincial, we find a bit more excitement in this university town. Koch has pointed out that Eckhart's being sent to Paris a second time by his Order was indeed a great honour. This is comparable to Thomas Aquinas, Master in Paris from 1256 to 1259, returning to teach there again from 1269 to 1272. However, I believe it was more than an honour. The Dominicans were putting some of their best minds in Paris to counter the hostilities against their deceased brother, Thomas Aquinas.[21]

The writings we have from this period of Eckhart's life include his commentaries on the Scriptures. These biblical works on the Book of Genesis, Exodus and the Gospel of John are scholastic works offering philosophical and spiritual reflections on the text. Maurer places Eckhart's questions on "motion" and the "death of Christ" during this period (1311–1314).[22] These treat the nature of change, particularly as it applies to Christ's dying upon the cross. Clearly, they are speculative works that push one's understanding of a thing's transformation. Their intention was very likely to support a Dominican position that was under attack. While it may be too complicated to explain here, it does deal with the nature of humanity in Christ. That is, it concerns the nature of the soul as uniquely one. While the issue is complicated, Eckhart found ways to convey a level of its meaning, even if not a precise technical understanding. Change in the soul will be a key concern in Eckhart's understanding of deiformity. We will discuss this later, but for now, it is best understood as how the human is transformed in holiness.

This was a popular concept among the Rhineland mystics, but it was fraught with theological dangers. To misunderstand could lead to an idea of multiple souls in the person, or a failure to appreciate the full potential of the person. Deiformity has to preserve the soul as unique, yet at the same time as distinct from the reality that is God. There is a remote chance that during this time Eckhart came to know about Marguerite of Porette, whose condemned work *The Mirror of Simple Souls* treated a similar theme. The Royal Inquisitor, the Dominican William of Paris, condemned her for failing to preserve this distinction between creature and Creator. She was burned at the stake as a heretic on June 1, 1310.

Eckhart's second and last stay in Paris was followed by his assignment to Strasbourg, where he would live for approximately ten years (1314–1324). This move placed him back in the southern German province of Teutonia.

Meister in Strasbourg

It is not clear when Eckhart's first name was lost to history, but most historians think it very likely was Johannes. What is clear is that after his time in Paris he was simply called Meister, or Master. Many people held him in high esteem and sought him out as a great preacher and master of the ways of God. In Strasbourg, Eckhart was involved in the care of Dominican nuns in the region. Biographical details for these years are scarce, but Koch does a praiseworthy job of tracking them down.[23] Not only was Eckhart a respected *magister* in the University of Paris, he was also a revered *Meister* of the spiritual life. The *lesemeister* (master of the text) was also the *lebemeister* (master of life), one who could bring high-minded concepts into the realities of life. Among his German followers, the name *Meister* gave the lofty academic title a more comfortable sound, for it meant a master at one's craft. Moreover, Eckhart's craft was the mysterious art of the Christian life.

With his many skills, Eckhart was given a special mission on behalf of the Dominican Order, a duty that gave him an honour greater than that of his prior. In November 1316, he acted as vicar on behalf of the Master of the Order, his old colleague from Paris, Berengar of Landora. Eckhart, in the name of the Master, negotiated a bequest given to the Dominican convent of nuns at St. Mark's in Strasbourg. Berengar, even before being elected Master of the Order, was a significant person of the times. He represented the University of Paris at the Council of Vienne (1311–1312), a council called by Pope Clement V (b. 1264/ reigned 1305–1314) under pressure from King Phillip IV of France, who wanted the Knights Templars condemned. This council took place while Eckhart was in Paris for his second stay as *Magister*. The Dominicans elected Berengar Master while he was still teaching in 1313, the year Eckhart ended his second stay in Paris. It made sense that Berengar would depute Eckhart and entrust him with some greater responsibilities, especially with the Dominican nuns. The climate in Strasbourg, as we will see, required very capable minds.

During these Strasbourg years, Eckhart delivered many of his German sermons. He was a frequent preacher at Dominican convents of nuns, which suggests that a special charge may have been given him on behalf of their protection. In 1318, the Pope elevated Berengar to the Episcopal See of Compostela in Spain (already a significant centre of pilgrimage). Consequently, in 1322 when the next Master, Herveus of France, was concerned with the convent in Unterleden, he sent Eckhart, along with friar Matthew of Finstingen, as his Visitators, or special envoys. Eckhart's abilities were well respected by two Masters of the Order and his role in Strasbourg was of some significance, but how?

The historian Francis Rapp[24] presents some insights into Strasbourg's cultural significance, wealth and political climate, which shed light on Eckhart's life. It seems that even in Strasbourg (like Cologne), a climate of concern existed in the face of false teaching or heterodoxy. One hundred years earlier, Pope Innocent III had condemned Ortlieb of Strasbourg for promoting Cathari beliefs; this was a form of Gnosticism that saw material existence as dualistic and sinful. The material and spiritual worlds were in conflict, and everything connected with matter, even physical procreation, was deemed sinful. This pitted the materially wealthy against the enlightened, who were poor in spirit, which made for conflicts in many towns. The Strasbourg of Eckhart's day experienced a resurgence of suspicions fired by pantheistic and lax elements promoted by the Brothers and Sisters of the Free Spirit.[25] These heterodox ideas may even have had an impact upon the Beguines and the cloistered nuns in Strasbourg.[26] Perhaps it was concern over this influence that Herveus decided to delegate a Master of Paris as his Visitator in Strasbourg. Another factor was an emerging *de facto* alliance between the mendicant orders and the patrician families that created further political tension for the bishop, Jean of Dirpheim.[27] The bishop was irritated by the Dominican mendicants, who provided protection to the Beguines and other lay groups. Eckhart's role as Dominican Visitator, or envoy, as well as a poor mendicant, put him in the midst of a brewing storm along the Rhine.

However, Eckhart's preaching and his ministerial care were not limited only to religious. His care for lay people is evident in his *Das Buch der göttlichen Tröstung* (*Book of Divine Consolation*), written for the grieving Queen Agnes of Hungary, whose father, King Albrecht I, was murdered in 1308; his sermon *"Von dem edlen menschen"* ("Of the Nobleman") was intended as an explanation of the inner life to the laity. So, even well into his sixties, Eckhart was a trusted servant of the Order, which makes the subsequent accusations made against him in Cologne all the more difficult to accept. Little did this godly man realize what twist of reason would corrupt his works. In the next chapter, we will look at this mystic's trial in Cologne.

2

A Godly Man

The Conflict

After 1324, we find that Eckhart is once more back in Cologne – the place where he had governed his new province a decade earlier – at the *studium generale* of his Order, a kind of university for Dominican men. The reason for sending him to Cologne is unclear; perhaps as a senior friar (then in his mid-sixties) it was to teach the young students there. It is during this time that he established his ties with two other Dominicans who were also teaching there: Johannes Tauler (d. 1361) and Heinrich Suso (d. 1366). Both

Tauler and Suso are well-known spiritual masters in their own right. Their work reveals that Eckhart influenced these two men very much.

The Cologne community no doubt shared the excitement of living with someone of Eckhart's calibre. It makes sense that his presence in Cologne was a valuable resource not only because he was a Master of Paris, but a spiritual master as well. It is likely that the community of Cologne encouraged Eckhart to compile some of his works, a collection that would later be known as the *Opus Tripartitum* (Three Part Work). He may have begun this project while still in Strasbourg, but it was in Cologne that he hoped to integrate his ideas. It was to be a great work, according to Eckhart's introduction, bringing together the Scriptures, Thomas Aquinas and the philosophers. It would have been a golden retirement; had he completed this work, our understanding of his mature thought would have been much richer. Sadly, Eckhart's time in Cologne did not allow for such an undertaking. In an almost tragic way, these last years were perhaps the most difficult ones of his entire life.

Here in the ancient Roman city and archiepiscopal see of Cologne stood the Dominican convent, just a short distance from the cathedral, which was then modest in size. The choir, begun in 1289, had just been dedicated in 1322. Legend has attributed its design to Albert the Great, but that was not the case. The episcopal palace was in Bonn; the Archbishop of Cologne was one of the Imperial Electors (the German term is *Kurfürsten*), a key political role in the Empire. Cologne was a wealthy and powerful diocese whose vote was one of seven able to elect the German king, which was preliminary to the king's accession as the Holy Roman Emperor. Their vote was most often used to resolve hereditary claims, which is exactly what happened in Eckhart's lifetime, with conflicts between the Staufer and Hapsburg dynasties.

We may never know the reasons for the conflict that entangled the Franciscan Archbishop of Cologne, Henry of Virneburg, and Meister Eckhart. Archbishop Virneburg was from a powerful family. The tenth of thirteen children born to Count Henry I and Princess Ponzetta of Oberstein, he was named Archbishop of Cologne at the age of 22 and ruled for 28 years. Perhaps the Dominicans were too close for Archbishop Henry, who appears in an unfavourable light throughout the literature. Did the Archbishop bear an old grudge against Eckhart? Or, was the tragedy in Cologne part of a larger drama? We may never know, but concerning this prince of the Church, the Archbishop of Cologne, one scholar has said,

> He was a hard man who made full use of the harsh treatment then customary in dealing with heretics. He was also at this time an old man, set in his ways, and was genuinely worried at the spread of heretical ideas.[1]

The Christendom of medieval Europe placed great importance on orthodoxy. Against superstition and ignorance, it seemed to provide some sense of direction. Robert E. Lerner, citing the *Concilia Germaniae* in his work *The Heresy of the Free Spirit in the Later Middle Ages*, also shows Henry to be a harsh man, especially concerning the beghards – laymen who begged or, more accurately in some cases, extorted alms, though they were not vowed religious. They preached a gospel of such personal freedom that they often opposed any obedience to the tradition of the Church. Lerner tells us:

> Henry [of Virneburg] was always concerned with discipline at any price and for such a man unregulated beghards were an obvious annoyance. Therefore, a year after his consecration in 1306, he included a decree directed against beghards of both sexes in a series of synodal decisions aimed at reforming the state of his diocese.[2]

Lerner also tells us of the kind of punishment this prelate of the Church employed. In one account, it seems that there was a priest of the Cologne diocese named Walter, who was found to be a heretic. The Archbishop had him defrocked and burned at the stake. Other heretics (including six women) were either imprisoned for life or, as one dubious report held, drowned in the Rhine.[3] The iron rule of this bishop would not tolerate any threat to orthodoxy and good order.

However, a more sympathetic reading justifies the Archbishop's fears in his diocese. There were numerous groups of women called "beguines" throughout the area – a new, popular lay women's movement inspired by ideals like those of the beghards: these women sought to live the poverty of Christ. While some of the beghards (the male counterpart) went so far as to reject the sacraments and the laws of the Church, declaring themselves spiritually free from such laws, the beguines were less radical. However, there was one way in which they were unconventional: they were not vowed religious and therefore lived beyond church structures and beyond the Archbishop's control. It was a very attractive model for noblewomen who wanted to live religiously while retaining the freedom to leave. Between 1300 and 1310, over 40 beguine communities of women were founded in Cologne, doubling the previous number.[4] These communities were walled towns within the city where women lived in prayer and simplicity, doing charitable works and sharing their wealth. While similar to the oblates in their lay status and pious devotion, they differed in their independence and autonomy from church institutions. They might be better understood as akin to the contemporary Catholic Worker Movement, meeting the social needs of their day, not obligated by vows but united by free association.

It is significant to recall that Eckhart was provincial from 1303 to 1311, during a time of growth in the beguine movement. Dominicans often defended these quasi-religious groups; we can assume Eckhart had dealings with Archbishop Henry on this issue. Fear of these movements had spread among people for various reasons. Recall that in 1310, the Royal Inquisitor had burned Marguerite of Porette in Paris for heresy and, as we saw, the return of unorthodox Cathari in Strasbourg made for a climate of suspicion. Stories circulated of nocturnal orgies, acts of homosexuality and obscene rituals happening in caverns beneath Cologne itself. One story in Lerner tells of a husband who trapped his wife by following her in disguise to such an orgy. He slipped her wedding band from her finger while there, and confronted her with it the next day. Given these and other stories, it is understandable that the Archbishop would act harshly to crush what he saw as sin and error in his diocese.

Not only were there scandalous situations pressing upon the Archbishop, but he also felt the press of a changing world triggered by natural catastrophes and political unrest. Lerner neatly captures the feeling of the period and its changes.

> What caused this shift?... [T]he orthodox were becoming more conservative and many idealists more radical. After the later thirteenth century the cult of poverty was more and more in question, the mendicant orders as a whole were on the defensive, and there was a growing distaste among ecclesiastics, both secular and regular, for lay pursuit of the apostolic life. On the other hand, the laity, who sought a life of perfection, were alienated by the flagging esprit of the orders and official lack of patience for bold experiments in lay piety. More than that, the calamities of the fourteenth century underscored dissatisfaction with established ways. The fourteenth century was a time of trauma in northern Europe...an age of adversity. In the first half of the century...the economy was reeling from falling agricultural yields, climatic disasters, the worst of which was the terrible flood of 1314–1315,

internecine wars, high taxes, shortage of bullion, and the contraction of trade routes, especially those to the East. There can be no doubt that men knew they were living in bad times.[5]

Lerner's treatment of politically turbulent Germany between 1314 and 1322 lends certain legitimacy to the prelate's concerns. The struggles of Emperor Ludwig of Bavaria with the Hapsburgs, the papacy, and France brought about anarchy as alliances shifted among the German princes. Ludwig (of the Staufen dynasty) declared himself Emperor without the Pope's required approval; the Pope, meanwhile, wanted the Hapsburg dynasty to continue their imperial rule. As one of the seven imperial electors, Archbishop Henry would have been equal to these German princes, along with the Archbishop of Mainz, Matthias of Bucheck (1321–28) and Archbishop of Trier, Baldwin of Luxemburg (1307–54). [These three archbishoprics were Archchancellors of the Empires of Italy (Cologne), Germany (Mainz), and Gaul (Trier).] Archbishop Henry's oldest brother, Ruprecht II's third son, who was also named Henry, would later become Archbishop Elector of Mainz (1328–46) at the age of eighteen.

The political climate of the day was also very unfortunate, as Pope John XXII and the German clergy sought to undermine Emperor Ludwig.[6] This in turn spawned anticlericalism from the crown that sought the suppression and destruction of monasteries; recall the Dominican Order's ongoing struggle to establish the Dortmund house. Those loyal to Ludwig also sought the humiliation of priests and imposed forced manual labour on the clergy. Pope John's strategy of Interdict, the custom of banning the celebration of the Church's rites in a region, was rigorous, as we see in Lerner's description:

John XXII knew very well what he was doing. In a letter of 1323 to the Archbishop of Cologne he predicted that the results of his interdict on all churches and localities that remained loyal to the Emperor would be that "corpses would lie unburied in piles for so long that their stink would infect the healthy; the innocent would have to go without the sacraments for so long that irreverence would grow; heresy would thrive and so would distress of soul...." None of this seemed to worry Christ's vicar, but even one of his Cardinals was moved in 1334 to implore him to become more flexible with the words, "Holy Father, believe me, this rigor may be lawful, but it is not expedient."[7]

It was amid all this tension that Eckhart returned to Cologne, and I have no doubt that these circumstances played their part in the tragedy that would unfold. Let us now focus our attention upon the final years of Eckhart's life, which entangled him in the pangs and pains of a world in labour.

Problems for the Cologne Dominicans

Koch[8] reports that the Dominican general chapter of Venice (1325) wanted to correct some of the brethren of Germany whose preaching had compromised the Order's position in the struggle between Pope John XXII, who supported the Hapsburg rival Frederick the Fair, and the Staufen self-crowned Emperor Ludwig of Bavaria. Since 1309, when Pope Clement V (1305–14) moved the papacy to a small papal territory in southern France known as Avignon, the politics of the Germans was of great concern. The German king was customarily the Holy Roman Emperor, holding territories in Italy. This situation often conflicted with papal plans, and in turn Emperor Ludwig opposed Pope John XXII. The two powerful religious Orders of the time were also drawn into the imperial-papal conflict. The Franciscans supported Emperor Ludwig, while the Dominicans were loyal to the Avignon Papacy and its excommunication of Ludwig in 1324. Consequently, the Dominican position in imperial Germany was vulnerable to political compromise. Recall that their property in the imperial city of Dortmund was still in contention.

Perhaps Eckhart's move to Cologne was part of a larger strategy to address legal and canonical concerns that he would know about from his time as provincial. It makes sense that this general political concern is the reason why Nicholas of Strasbourg as well as Benedict of Asnago were dispatched to Cologne by the Dominican Order. Nicholas had been a lector or professor in Cologne at the *studium generale*. If the Chapter sent Eckhart to Cologne as a kind of expert in these matters, his reputation would be his chief currency. Given the sequence of events, we know that rumours attacking Eckhart's orthodoxy circulated in Cologne at this time; we cannot help but assume that they may have been aimed to discredit Eckhart. In this climate, it would have been politically expedient for Nicholas, possibly in anticipation of Archbishop Henry of Virneburg's concerns, to investigate Eckhart's teachings. Nicholas's internal investigation found no errors in Eckhart's theology, and in the eyes of the Order, this cleared him of any suspicion. Given the heightened – one might even say paranoid – concerns in Cologne, the theological nuances that were appreciated in Strasbourg or by a sympathetic reader were lost among the Cologne ecclesiastics. The Archbishop of Cologne did not give much weight to this "in-house" scrutiny and instituted an episcopal process against Eckhart in early 1326.

This move on the part of the Archbishop was, I believe, calculated. It called into question the Dominican Order's review and cast a shadow of doubt on the Dominicans in Cologne. His exact motives are unclear, but it is difficult to deny that political strategies seem more likely than questions of orthodoxy, especially after Nicholas's investigation. This action, it would seem, directly questioned the integrity of the Dominican investigation. In the end, it transferred control of the entire matter into the Archbishop's realm of canonical power. Koch has recounted that in the first appeal to the Pope (January 14, 1327), the Archbishop's Commission disparagingly identified Nicholas as a "lector friar" of the Dominican house in Cologne, implying some conflict of interests regarding Eckhart. Furthermore, the Commission held, Koch points out, that

> Nicholas was still Lector in 1327...[and] Lector Nicholas was subordinate to Master Eckhart. As Vicar of the General and Visitator of Teutonia, Nicholas stood over him, with the task of testing the orthodoxy of his teaching. He was, apart from Eckhart, the only theological expert at the Cologne General Studium. It is under these circumstances neither astonishing that Nicholas defended the orthodoxy of his Master, nor that the prosecutors appointed by the Archbishop were sceptical about the defence.[9]

A case may be made in defence of the Archbishop's scepticism. It seems the "malicious" testimony against Eckhart by Hermann of Summo and William of Nidecken, two discontented Dominicans,[10] further fed the Archbishop's suspicion. Their testimony created reasonable doubt on to the situation in the Dominican community and the obvious tensions in Cologne. Furthermore, Nicholas, the official Visitator, had earlier censored these two malcontents. Here is the question for their motive: was it retaliation or concern for religious orthodoxy? As if this intrigue were not enough, the Cologne tribunal brought counter-charges against Nicholas because of these two malcontents. The actions in Cologne all seem designed to undermine the Dominicans.

The Process and Trials

The charge of heresy was a serious and effective means to undo an opponent. Unlike the sensationalized notions surrounding local trials of wrongly accused heretics (such as Joan of Arc almost 200 years later), the canonical or ecclesial process sought to defend orthodoxy. The accused was able to defend his or her case before a tribunal. If found guilty, the accused could renounce his or her false doctrine and be reconciled with the Church. If the accused refused to do so, a variety of ecclesiastical sanctions could be invoked. Death was for capital crimes and was the secular arm's responsibility. In Eckhart's case, as we will see, there were many more variables at work. These had to do with his rights as a university professor and as a Dominican.

Bernard McGinn has provided an analysis of Eckhart's trial, bringing together the works of three prominent scholars.[11] McGinn presents "a review of the course of the two trials, an analysis of the theological principles of Eckhart's Defense, and an evaluation of the meaning of the final condemnation."[12] Rather than duplicating McGinn's work, we shall make use of his research on the trials of Cologne and Avignon along with Koch's work.

So, what was it that set Henry of Virneburg against Meister Eckhart and the Dominicans? Alternatively, was it the commission with the axe to grind? Concerning the Archbishop's commission, McGinn writes:

> It was apparently in the early part of 1326 that the episcopal process was formally begun under two inquisitors, Reiner Friso, a canon of the cathedral and *magister*, and the Franciscan Peter of Estate [later replaced by another Franciscan, Albert of Milan]. The method followed was one which had been used for centuries but had become increasingly standardized since 1270, the extraction of excerpts, or *articuli*, from the works of the accused and their organization into lists called *rotuli*.[13]

Most of us can see the difficulties with such a process that excludes the context and nuances of a proposition. However, the commission's purpose was to expose every shred of erroneous teaching found in Eckhart. The process extracted from Eckhart's writings just those passages that seemed heretical, excluding from it what might have suggested an orthodox interpretation. The goal was to render down the heretical propositions to which the accused would offer a response.

McGinn further relays that in Eckhart's case there were two *rotuli*: one containing 49 articles taken from his Latin and German works, the other having 59 drawn exclusively from Eckhart's vernacular German sermons. The vernacular sermons present a special case because these were not manuscripts written by Eckhart but recorded renditions made by his auditors or listeners. Those who heard him preach wrote down his sermons, perhaps to share with others or to preserve a record of what he had said. This process produced over one hundred propositions that were deemed suspect. Furthermore, an additional *rotuli* against Eckhart seems possible. Most likely formulated in Cologne, it demonstrates "a concern for verbal precision rather than free paraphrase, as well as a length that seems to indicate some passion for complete coverage."[14] These articles were presented to the accused, who then had to give a response to them in writing.

We possess a declaration given by Eckhart on September 26, 1326. This was three years after Aquinas's canonization, a fact that did not escape Eckhart. The charge of heresy was brought against Aquinas, only later to have him declared a saint. Eckhart said,

> I, the aforesaid Brother Eckhart of the order of Preachers, respond. First, I protest before you the Commissioners, Master Reiner Friso, Doctor of Theology, and Peter of Estate, lately Custodian of the order of Friars Minor, that according to the exemption and privileges of my order, I am not held to appear before you or to answer charges. This is especially so since I am not accused of heresy and have never been denounced overtly, as my whole life and teaching testify, and as the esteem of the brethren of the whole order and men and women of the entire kingdom and of every nation corroborates. Second, it is evident from this that the commission given you by the venerable father and lord, the Archbishop of Cologne (may God preserve

his life!), has no force inasmuch as it proceeds from a false suggestion and an evil root and stem. Indeed, if I were less well known among the people and less eager for justice, I am sure that such attempts would not have been made against me by envious people. But I ought to bear them patiently, because "Blessed are they who suffer for justice's sake"(Mt. 5:10), and according to Paul, "God scourges every son he receives"(Heb. 12:6), so that I can deservedly say with the Psalm, "I have been made ready in scourges"(Ps. 37:18). I ought to do this particularly because long ago, but in my own lifetime, the masters of theology at Paris received a command from above to examine the books of those two most distinguished men, Saint Thomas Aquinas and Brother Albert the Bishop, on the grounds that they were suspect and erroneous. Many have often written, declared and even publicly preached that Saint Thomas wrote and taught errors and heresies, but with God's aid his life and teaching alike have been given approval, both at Paris and also by the Supreme Pontiff and the Roman curia.[15]

What stands out in the declaration is the importance the Meister gives to his life and doctrine. The tragic circumstance behind this document and its content is more than a defence and, as such, it merits a fuller discussion. McGinn, citing Théry, says, "He prefaced this document with a denial of the competency of the court to hear his case, appealing to the pope or the University of Paris as the only tribunals that could judge theological matters that did not touch the faith."[16] While McGinn's points are true, his comments seem to overlook one key aspect of Eckhart's words. Eckhart's denial of the commissioners' right to have him appear before them and answer their questions is premised first upon the legal grounds of his Order's "exemption and privileges." This suggests that Eckhart was mindful of a larger canonical concern. It is about two legitimate privileges, which trumped the Cologne tribunal's jurisdiction. More significantly, it would be a challenge to the Archbishop's jurisdiction itself. This is immediately followed by an appeal to a higher truth warranted in the facts when he says, "this is especially true." Here Eckhart gives three significant elements: 1) the *fact* that he has never been accused or denounced of heresy, 2) the *reality* of the testimony of his whole life and teaching (an argument which is cited later in his reference to Aquinas), and 3) the *evidence* of universal esteem (in the Order, the kingdom and every nation). Not only does Eckhart draw from these facts his exemption from the commission, but he also denies the force of the commission, since it proceeds from something evil, the evil of "envious people."[17] Here is where we might wonder about the people Eckhart references. Was it just the envy of the Dominican malcontents that implicated Eckhart and Nicholas? Was it Archbishop Henry's desire to have absolute control that motivated him to eliminate all threats? Or was there a larger social cause to be found in those loyal to imperial policies? Regardless of the source, it is significant that Eckhart sees envy as the culprit.

Here we find an important and revealing characteristic of Eckhart. Rather than absolutely rejecting the commission's demands, Eckhart bears them, or at least is aware of the moral necessity to bear them, and to do so patiently. Here is the depth of Eckhart; here the man of profound prayer lets go to the God who calls him to *suffer for justice* (Mt. 5:10), who *renews him in this suffering* (Heb. 12:6), and *readies him in suffering* (Ps. 37:18). Eckhart cited all these Scripture texts in his defence. His appeal to the words of Scriptures is not as dead words in some book, but as living words, which he experienced and which gave meaning to his life and teaching. Living words, which vindicated the life and teaching of Thomas and Albert, and which he believed would be his vindication as well. This, I believe, is extremely important, for it demonstrates the unity of the master of the text and the master of life. Eckhart's life and teaching should not be seen as limited to this particular moment of a commission void of force and power, but rather seen in the powerful voice of Scripture, tradition and history: that is to say, his whole life. This is by no means a resignation or flight from life, but is best understood as an embracing of life. It is what Eckhart himself called "unattachment" (*abgeschiedenheit*).

This notion of unattachment may be seen as the central theme of Eckhart's final years. Unfortunately, many have translated it as "detachment." It is so ingrained in the literature that it is pointless to try to ignore it. I am afraid that we are stuck using it. Though we are left using the word "detachment," Eckhart's meaning is something richer, and that we can try to convey. If we understand this notion as detachment is commonly taken, we run the risk of conveying a sense of disdain or rejection. This is not what Eckhart means. We do not need to reject dualistically the world; rather, we ought not to be controlled by it. Detachment can also convey a sense of our own subjective detaching, my choosing to be detached, which is not Eckhart's point. He is more interested in how we are not attached to created things so we can be open to knowing their Creator. A spirit of holy detachment was present in his attitude toward the trial. Eckhart does not see suffering and humility as his defeat, but as the activity of God. God, who is supreme detachment, is the one purifying, cleansing, enkindling, awakening, stimulating, showing, separating and uniting. This is the God of the living and the life centring of Eckhart the *lebemeister*. Eckhart's "unattachment," which is present in his reaction to the commission and overlooked by so many historians, reveals an essential piece of the Eckhart picture. The Meister, in the final chapter of his work *On Detachment*, had this to say:

> So detachment is the best of all, for it purifies the soul and cleanses the conscience and enkindles the heart and awakens the spirit and stimulates our longings and

shows us where God is and separates us from created things and unites itself with God. Now, all you reasonable people take heed! The fastest beast that will carry you to your perfection is suffering [*lîden*], for no one will enjoy more eternal sweetness than those who endure with Christ in the greatest bitterness. There is nothing more gall-bitter than suffering, and nothing more honey-sweet than to have suffered [*geliten-hân*]; nothing disfigures the body more than suffering, and nothing more adorns the soul in the sight of God than to have suffered. The firmest foundation on which this perfection can stand is humility, for whichever mortal crawls here in the deepest abasement, his spirit will fly up into the highest realms of the divinity, for love brings sorrow, and sorrow brings love. Therefore, whoever longs to attain to perfect detachment [*swer begert ze kommenne ze volkomener abegescheidenheit*], let him struggle for perfect humility, and so he will come close to divinity.[18]

We cannot underestimate the significance this idea plays in our present attempts to understand Eckhart's life and learning. As the passage suggests, Eckhart's sense of human suffering acknowledged its grotesqueness; yet he saw in the present perfect state of "having suffered" something that draws one close to divinity itself. This was possible because of this perfect detachment, which enables us to see the value even in the reality of suffering, to see beyond the created order. This perspective allowed Eckhart to face the realities of his final years, to see the divine even in his sufferings.

The Avignon Appeal

It was quite an ordeal for Eckhart as the process dragged on. Early in January 1327, four months after Eckhart's formal defence, the commission cited Nicholas of Strasbourg for impeding the process. Nicholas, the official Visitator, had issued three protests to the commission. In his complaint, he repeated the challenge to their competency and made appeal to take the case to the Pope. Nicholas suspected the veracity of two witnesses, who were discontented Dominicans.

A change of venue would be more sympathetic to the Dominican Order, and it was the Order's right to such a papal
hearing. Both the Franciscan and Dominican Orders had been
granted a special dispensation from the Church allowing them
pontifical arbitration. This safeguard against local judgments
was not uncommon. The faculty at the University of Paris held
a similar right to be judged by their fellow theologians and
not municipal or provincial authorities. Eckhart himself filed
a similar protest on January 24 of the same year. One of his
concerns reflected the scandal to the clergy and laity brought
on by the lengthy process, affecting not only himself but the
Order as well. Clearly, the fallout was of greater consequence
than to just Eckhart's reputation.

On February 13, 1327, Eckhart further stressed his position when he preached in Cologne. No doubt he was eager
to end the matter. Koch informs us of Eckhart's conciliatory
attitude and innocence:

> He declares his disgust against all heresy and all moral
> errors, and agrees to revoke any of his writings, sayings
> or preaching as far as it would prove to be incompat-
> ible with sound church teaching. And he particularly
> makes his defence against three points on which he
> had been misunderstood.[19]

This was an effort on the part of Eckhart to satisfy any concern as to his orthodoxy and a willingness to redress anything
contrary to Church teaching. Koch finds Eckhart's statement
very embarrassing, saying, "It is recourse to public opinion
which could have had no hope of a favourable outcome."[20]
However, I wonder if public opinion wasn't the underlying
reason. Eckhart was concerned about the scandal of his case to
the laity and the damaging impact this was having on the Dominican Order. What better forum to declare his willingness
to submit to orthodox teaching than the Dominican church in
Cologne, and to demand his right to papal judgment? In February, the archdiocesan commission refused Eckhart's appeal,

but this was a mere formality. The Archbishop was forced to let the case go to the Papal Court in Avignon, but Koch notes with irony that the upper hand ultimately may have been given to the Archbishop by this move.[21] It is not clear what Koch meant but there seem to be two possible advantages. First, Eckhart was no longer in Cologne and no longer an obstacle to the Archbishop's plans. Second, the case before the Papal Court would be alongside several prominent cases brought against the Franciscans. Given Archbishop Henry's nephew's appointment as Archbishop Elector of Mainz the following year (1328), one wonders if this may have given Virneburg's family a political advantage as well.

Eckhart went to Avignon to defend his case before the Pope. Escorted by Dominicans who would witness on his behalf, he journeyed from Cologne to the Dominican house in Avignon. Travel was easier when one followed trade routes, and Cologne was a hub of trade. The Rhine River was the chief passageway for Europe from Holland north of Cologne and on south to Basel. From there it was a relatively simple journey to Avignon, and a positive spirit seems to have been present among Eckhart and his supporters. Koch writes,

> Concerning the result of the process against Eckhart an optimistic sense prevailed in the early summer of 1327 as one can read from the remark that no one who knew Eckhart's life could doubt his faith and holy way of life.[22]

To most people the entire fiasco must have seemed incredible. Surely, the great teacher and master would be vindicated, or so they hoped.

Pope John XXII, at that time entangled with the politics of the German emperor, Ludwig of Bavaria, set up a commission to examine the evidence sent from Cologne. Cardinal Fournier, himself a Master of the University of Paris (later to become Pope Benedict XII), may have played a moderating role in the investigations. Fournier, a talented Cistercian theologian, served John XXII on many inquisitorial matters. He was so prominent an adviser to the Pope that he had been made a Cardinal Priest in 1327. Because he enjoyed such papal favour, it is very likely that he was given charge of the Eckhart case. This was one case among several under consideration at Avignon. In 1326, John XXII had condemned a work by the Franciscan Peter John Olivi (d. 1298), and in 1327 John XXII had summoned the Franciscan Master General to Avignon: both cases concerned Franciscan poverty and the Spiritual Franciscans who were critical of ecclesiastical wealth. This movement condemned the Church's wealth and advocated day-to-day begging as true to Christ's poverty. In retaliation, the Franciscan theologian William of Ockham declared Pope John XXII heretical.

All in all, the Avignon phase of Eckhart's case seems to have been characterized by genuine concern for the faith. McGinn points out that the selective editing of the *rotuli* from Cologne took place within a process that was very thorough. He writes,

> Pope John eventually received two reports on the matter of Eckhart. The one that survives to us, the *Gutachten*, that is the *votum theologicum* of the full commission, probably dates from 1327. This interesting document not only shows that the unwieldy mass of articles from the original *rotuli* had been carefully pruned down to a manageable group of twenty-eight (the same articles that were to appear in the Papal Bull), but it also displays considerable theological skill in its rebuttal of the Meister's arguments. The form of the document follows a reverse model of the scholastic *quaestio*: each suspect article is taken as the statement of an orthodox position, reasons are then given for the error of this view, the Meister's defense of the position is summarized, and finally decisive rejoinders are given to his arguments.[23]

The integrity of Eckhart's case was required, given the political climate, but more likely it was due to Cardinal Fournier's own sense of theological thoroughness.

Sometime before April 30, 1328, Eckhart died.[24] The exact time and place are unknown, but we do possess a letter from the Pope to Archbishop Henry of Cologne guaranteeing the continuation of the trial in spite of Eckhart's death. He may have died as early as the fall of 1327, but this seems unlikely. On March 27, 1329, Pope John issued the bull *In Agro Domi-nico*, which condemned a total of twenty-eight articles (two of which were not Eckhart's).[25] The bull, however, does not condemn Eckhart or his other orthodox teachings. In fact, the bull takes great effort to state expressly Eckhart's fidelity to the Church "at the end of his life." Pope John XXII wrote:

> Further, we wish it to be known both to those among whom these articles were preached or taught, and to any others to whose notice they have come, that the aforesaid Eckhart, as is evident from a public document drawn up for that purpose, professed the Catholic faith at the end of his life and revoked and also deplored the twenty-six articles, which he admitted that he had preached, and also any others, written and taught by him, whether in the schools or in sermons, insofar as they could generate in the minds of the faithful a heretical opinion, or one erroneous and hostile to the true faith. He wished them to be considered absolutely and totally revoked, just as if he had revoked the articles and other matters severally and singly by submitting both himself and everything that he had written and preached to the judgment of the Apostolic See and our own judgment.[26]

Edmund Colledge[27] has made the bold observation concerning this final paragraph of the bull that nowhere does it mention that these propositions were considered heretical by Eckhart himself. It is suggested that he rejected the false understandings that could lead one to heretical belief, but not their fundamental tenets. This reveals a man who faced his death, as Colledge puts it, "unyielding." I am inclined to see this as Eckhart, ever the Dominican, making the distinctions Truth demands.

This summary may give the impression that the Eckhart matter was only a local concern between the archbishop and a theologian, but this was not the case. The interest of the Franciscans in Eckhart's case suggests a wider circle of political concern. The result of the papal proceedings may have been relayed by Archbishop Henry to the Franciscan Minister General, Michael of Cesena. In late May, Michael of Cesena had fled from Avignon with Bonogratia of Bergamo and William of Ockham (who had been kept at Avignon under house arrest since 1324), arriving in Pisa on June 9. They obtained protection from the self-proclaimed Emperor Ludwig of Bavaria. This action formed a schismatic Franciscan group in Munich. In an attempt to undermine the papal forces, the Franciscan Minister General wrote from Pisa in September of 1328 a letter deriding the Dominican heresies of Eckhart, and Nicholas of Strasbourg's defence of him.[28] These are indications that the troubles between Archbishop Henry of Cologne and the Dominican Eckhart were not just a matter of local politics, but part of a larger papal-imperial conflict. Furthermore, the weight of the condemnation is mollified by John XXII's letter (April 1329) to the Archbishop of Cologne authorizing the bull's limited publication to the Cologne diocese and ecclesiastical province.[29] In effect, this limited the bull to the Cologne territory, as if to say it was of minor significance.

There is some further circumstantial evidence that seems to link the case of Ockham with that of Eckhart. In 1324, the Pope summoned William of Ockham to Avignon where John Lutterell, former chancellor of Oxford University (1317–1322), had denounced Ockham as a heretic. Ockham promoted an early form of nominalism that denied the existence of universals; thus he eliminated God's sovereignty. Ockham taught that universals were not divinely instituted but are nothing more than human concepts, something that we humans construct. In this same year, 1324, Eckhart returned to Cologne, a powerful elector city, under the ecclesial juris- diction of the Franciscan Archbishop, in imperial Germany, which had already suffered from the papal interdict. Back in Avignon, Pope John XXII had appointed six theologians to examine Ockham. Among the six was John Lutterell, already set against Ockham, and Durandus of Saint Pourçain, a Dominican.

Whether Durandus was sympathetic toward Ockham's case may not be the significant question; rather, the political fallout of the papal actions may hold the key. In 1326, this commission presented 51 propositions against Ockham, the same year the episcopal process in Cologne began its inves- tigation of Eckhart. A coincidence on the surface, but one wonders if these two trials are not linked. In late 1326, the head of the Franciscan Friars Minor, Michael of Cesena, was summoned to Avignon and detained there, while in early Janu- ary of 1327 the Dominican Visitator, Nicholas of Strasbourg, was cited by the Cologne commission. In addition, in 1327 William of Ockham drew up counter-charges against John XXII, arguing that the Pope had forfeited his right to be pope for having lapsed into heresy. Circumstances in Germany were not favourable for Dominicans who throughout supported the Pope against the Emperor. Ludwig of Bavaria was at odds with the Pope, in turn the Pope refused to recognize Ludwig's election as emperor. This lack of an emperor meant that the vacant throne fell under papal rule. It was in 1327 that the Dominicans succeeded in having the Cologne proceedings, with the help of the papal court, transferred to Avignon. Later this same year the papal commission presented a list of 28 articles against Eckhart. The Pope turned these articles over to Cardinal Jacques Fournier for his opinion. In May 1328,

Michael of Cesena, Ockham and others fled to Pisa, territory under the Emperor's protection. This may have been a calculated move to discredit Pope John XXII, since the Emperor had just named a Franciscan in Rome as the anti-pope, Nicholas V (1328–30). While somewhat circumstantial, there are enough "loose threads" to warrant the suspicion that something more must be behind the Eckhart trial. Allow me to explain.

In light of what has been said, the actions of Pope John XXII to limit the circulation of the bull *In agro Dominico* may not have stemmed from local concerns. When we set this action against the backdrop of (1) a Franciscan bishop's (Henry of Virneburg) accusations against a Dominican, (2) whose Order supported the Avignon Papacy against the Emperor, and (3) a disloyal minister general of the Franciscans (4) living under the protection of an enemy of the Church, the excommunicated Emperor (5) who just had a Franciscan, Pietro Rainalducci elected as antipope (Nicholas V), certainly one is permitted to wonder at the politics of the bull's containment. One of the most fascinating things about history is not what we know but what is left in the shadows of time. In the end, we may know very little of Eckhart's final years. What we do know suggests a man linked to an amazing and intriguing conflict of ecclesiastical and imperial politics.

The trial of Eckhart, his years as provincial and his two terms as a Master at the University of Paris are hardly part of the common notion we have of a mystic. Yet these realities of life are as much the mystic we call Meister Eckhart as are his many writings. His ability to cut through the distraction and noise of life, getting people to tune into their essential ground, is the truly mystical element in Meister Eckhart. That essential ground is the humanizing and humane essence of the person to whom Jesus points us. It is this reality that Eckhart called *grunt*, the ground.

To this day, ironically, the ground of Eckhart's final resting – where he died and his burial place – is unknown. Emperor

Ludwig, William of Ockham and Michael of Cesena all died in Munich, and Pope John XXII died in Avignon, but Eckhart's death and burial remain a mystery. History, in a poetic sense, has kept hidden what Eckhart believed to be the most profound aspect of the person, the ground of their existence. Is he buried in Avignon, the place of his final trial? Was he brought by the entourage back to Germany, to Strasbourg, or Erfurt, or Cologne? History has sealed her lips, at least for now, and we must seek the man's mystical ground: not where he is buried but where he is most alive.

It is that ground in Eckhart's life that we have just explored. With this sense of Eckhart's life and times, we begin to understand the great wisdom guiding this mystic. Anyone who does not know anything about Eckhart, who presumes him to be some other-worldly character, will find the intriguing set of events and the politically astute life of this Meister out of character. But that is the point! The "who" of the mystic, the essence of the person, is far more the mystical dimension than is the "what," the non-essential things. Mystic is exactly who Eckhart was. His understanding of our call to Christian perfection begins with the reality of human life and the very principle of human life: the soul. In Part II, I will examine Eckhart's understanding of the soul: what I see as his Christian anthropology.

PART II

The Soul, De Anima

The first-time reader of Eckhart can find his ideas confusing. Many of the concepts are unfamiliar to the modern mind. However, I am surprised to find that those who have read something about him, or who have come across him in one way or another, often have a harder time with Eckhart. It may be that they read something about his idea of "letting-go," or "breaking-through," or "the birthing of God," or "the spark of the Divine." It may be that they are into Zen Buddhism or po-mo deconstructive theories. It may also be that they were on a retreat where Eckhart was used, or saw some inspiring passage in a greeting card. No matter how people first meet Eckhart, I am always curious to discover their understanding of one thing: Eckhart's sense of the soul.

This might seem an odd point, but if a reader lacks an appreciation of the soul in Eckhart, then it is difficult to appreciate him. All of his ideas are ultimately about the soul and its relation to God. This is true of his scholastic Latin writings, his commentaries and sermons on the Scriptures, as well as his *Parisian Questions*. However, it is especially true of his German writings, his sermons and treatises. Why is this concept of the soul so important for the person trying to understand Eckhart? It is important because in it we see how Eckhart understands the human person: his Christian anthropology.

Who are we? Why do we exist? These are fundamental philosophical and theological questions. They force us to examine our purpose in life, the direction and destiny that ground us. It is in confronting these kinds of questions that we see the genuinely human dimension of life striving toward some ultimate purpose or goal.

Consequently, Part II sets out Eckhart's basic understanding of the soul, starting in Chapter 3. It is through our coming to know the truest self that we are transformed into something divine. Eckhart's notion of deiformity, a person's conforming to this underlying reality of Godliness, is critical in his understanding of person, his understanding of the soul. Chapter 4 turns to the *exempla* or illustrations used by Eckhart in teaching people about the life of the soul. Over the years, I have found that Eckhart's own illustrations help to explain some of his very complex ideas. His understanding of the soul is developed using the same illustrations he found valuable. In doing this, the person trying to understand Eckhart will appreciate his fundamental starting point: the human person.

3

Eckhart's Christian Anthropology

Introduction

For a medieval thinker like Eckhart, any talk about the human soul implies what today we would call a "Christian anthropology." To be able even to talk about concepts like the soul requires a special kind of language. This special language is called Metaphysics, and the concept that we call "soul" is a metaphysical one. In Eckhart's day, "soul" sought to name the truest reality of being human, our ultimate destiny. In the neo-Platonic view, the soul was the most divine aspect of a person and therefore the noblest dimension of humanity.

Eckhart shared this notion and even refers to something in the soul that is the highest, noblest, purest thing about us: the *apex mentis* or *scintilla animae* ("spark of the soul").

Our modern filters hear the word "soul" in a dualistic way. On the one hand, it is somehow opposed to the "body." On the other hand, we think of it as so spiritual and occult as to make it beyond belief. This is why a modern reader of Eckhart needs to appreciate what the concept of soul really meant for Eckhart. The best modern equivalent for the word "soul" needs to express whatever it is that makes a person fully human. In the context of the Christian faith, we can speak of this context as a Christian anthropology, often referred to by Vatican II as the "dignity of the human person." From the point of view of Christ's Incarnation, "it" (whatever we call "it") is what makes a person fully human. Today, a discussion on this topic of Christian anthropology, addressing the concept of the soul, would make sense to Eckhart. Sadly, this profound dimension of the person is often overlooked in our materialistic society. We like to think that it does not really matter. And yet, there is an explosion of self-help spiritualities addressing our desire to find something more in the person. There really is something at work in the depths of human existence that cannot be proven, or ought not to be ignored. For this reason, one needs to read Eckhart in light of his larger anthropology, an incarnational anthropology that joins heaven and earth, the sacred and the secular.

Odd as the word "soul" may sound to our modern ears, perhaps as strange as the archaic "thee" and "thou," the language of the soul offers us a profound theological and anthropological lexicon, or a basic vocabulary of meanings. Aquinas tells us, "God is the spiritual life of the soul, as the soul is the life of the body."[1] Read that statement again: "God is the spiritual life of the soul, as the soul is the life of the body." Such a correlation between God and our human existence ought not to be dismissed as metaphysical poppycock. The fact is that the

traditional Christian language of the soul suggests an understanding of human existence far richer in depth and meaning.
Our modern ego-centred anthropology is often limited by
notions of self-actualized potentiality, while traditionally the
soul has been the *locus* or place for divine action in the person
who is open to being so acted upon. Words have the power
to name reality. The medieval fascination with a word's relationship to reality is akin to the same era's preoccupation with
distinctions. The development of a theological vocabulary
that opened the mind to amazing possibilities far beyond the
physical world was charged with excitement, just as quantum
physics provides an exciting new way of looking at our world.
Anyone who has lived abroad knows the power of language.
Putting one's thoughts and experience into words that one can
share with someone else is remarkable. A vocabulary about
the spiritual depth of human life is no less exciting. What soul
terminology provides for Christianity is a way of treating the
incarnate nearness of God, while still preserving the absolute
transcendence of God. We call this a paradox, and such language is challenging. It creates a tension in our imagination,
stretching the mind so we can glimpse a new reality.

Augustine is one of the great spiritual authorities in the
Christian West. His understanding of God as having left us
a vestige or footprint of the Trinity on the very makeup of
the human soul has inspired Christian authors for generations. However, Augustine's sense of God's nearness is always
matched by the paradoxical absolute awayness of God. In Book
6 of his *Confessions*, Augustine writes, "For you, O highest and
nearest, most hidden and most present, have no parts greater
and smaller. You are wholly everywhere, yet nowhere" (*Conf.* 6,
3). This way of speaking both fascinates and confounds us.

Aquinas, too, held this connection between God, the soul
and our bodily human existence. This divine nearness takes on
added social significance when we place it next to Thomas's
tract on Charity. For Aquinas, with whom Eckhart funda-

mentally agrees, the essential unity of soul and body gives greater importance to the existing reality of a person's life, specifically a person's living the virtuous life. Here we need to stress that the Christian understanding of soul is significantly different from other religions and philosophies on this point of immanence and transcendence. It is most important that we preserve the human soul as the active principle that unites and integrates the whole of a person's life. It integrates our material and physical realities as well as our non-material, non-physical realities – what we might call mental or spiritual realities. The soul does not simply unify the body: it is the integrating and unifying principle of all of one's individual and social relationships. It unifies our past, our present and our future. It integrates our present moment in human destiny. It is an active reality that holds together the unique and divinely created reality of a person.

If these ideas sound mystical, that is because they are. Truly, the reality of the human soul is ineffable; but that does not mean it is any less real. The work of these distant writers forged a way to name this soul reality that is still valuable today. Thomas Merton, the twentieth-century American Trappist monk, was familiar with this soul reality. In his 1972 work, *New Seeds of Contemplation,* he wrote:

> Every moment and every event of every person's life on earth plants something in one's soul. For just as the wind carries thousands of invisible and visible winged seeds, so the stream of time brings with it the germs of spiritual vitality that come to rest imperceptibly in the minds and wills of all.[2]

As I have said, the idea of the soul is a basic concept necessary for understanding Eckhart. This chapter treats Eckhart's Christian anthropology as found in his preaching. What better place for a Dominican to proclaim the perfection of what it means to be human? It is in his preaching to the people of his day that we find Eckhart's basic understanding

89

of the soul, its characteristics and its "life," the inner life as well as the outer life of the soul. It is for the salvation of souls that the Dominican Order exists, and it was to that end that Eckhart worked.

A Basic Understanding of the Soul

When we hear the word "soul," we often see it as opposed to the body. As we discussed, this is called dualism and has done much damage throughout history. In part, it is why many people have an unhealthy understanding of their body and human sexuality. It is also the reason why people think in black-and-white categories of good versus bad, heaven or hell, salvation or damnation. This antagonistic way of thinking forces us to see the body and soul at odds, locked in conflict. But how are the soul and body related to one another? What are the moral consequences of that relationship? These were the kind of questions Eckhart pondered.

For most of us, ideas about the soul do not enter into our daily conversations, so to appreciate Eckhart we will need a basic introduction. With our post-1960s, sexual-revolution understanding of our bodies, we mistrust the idea of a soul as somehow oppressive. However, Eckhart did not live in our times, and his sense of the body was quite different. For him, the body was not an end in itself but a means to something. He lived long before MRIs, plastic surgery and liposuction. For him, the body was a wondrous thing, guided on its way by the soul. It was something made holy because God was made flesh in Christ and God dwells among us in our humanity.[3]

From the time of Plato and before, people sought to explain why creatures differed one from another. How is it that human creatures seemed to reach a summit, at least in this world, of so many perfections? Eckhart clearly knows the thought of Plato and Aristotle, but he reveals a special familiarity with Aristotle's *De Anima (On the Soul)*. Not only that, but as a professor at the University of Paris, Eckhart was knowledgeable of how various master theologians and philosophers understood the human soul. Augustine, pseudo-Denis, Albert the Great, Thomas Aquinas, Bonaventure, Avicenna, Plotinus, Proclus and Maimonides all had slightly different takes on this subject. It is a challenge to think how a preacher might convey so complex a reality to his or her listeners today, let alone how Eckhart attempted to address his audience almost 700 years ago. Yet in many of his German sermons, he speaks of the soul. Four sermons in particular help us get a basic understanding of the soul: sermons 7, 14, 61 and 56.[4] Taken together, they give us a better sense of how Eckhart understands the soul. First, let's examine Eckhart's non-dualistic sense of the soul.

In Sermon 7, Eckhart brings together the texts of Hosea 14:4[5] ("Lord be mercy to the people that are in you"), and Luke 7:36-50. This gospel passage begins with a Pharisee's desire to have Jesus eat with him. However, the focus shifts when a woman, a known sinner, anoints the feet of Jesus. The story is one of mercy, which sends the sinner forth in peace. In his preaching on this passage, Eckhart employs both the Pharisee's desire to feast with Jesus and Jesus' words to the woman, "Go in peace," to establish the goal of human existence, that goal which is in Christ.

Here Eckhart illustrates the body's relationship to the soul with the theme of eating. Yes, eating. When we eat, the food we eat is united to our body. This unity of being is a crucial point in Eckhart. No longer can one distinguish the apple or roast: they are united with the body in one being (*Sein*), just as the body and soul are united in one being. To demonstrate how perfect this unity is, Eckhart distinguishes between a unity of being (i.e., what I eat and my body) and a unity of act (i.e., what my eye sees and what I perceive in my mind). He tells his listeners:

> The food, which I eat, is thus united with my body as my body is united with my soul. My body and my soul are united in one being, not as one act (as my soul unites itself with the eye in one action that is seeing). Thus, the food, which I eat, is not united in one act but in one being with my nature, which signifies the great union we shall have with God in one being, not in one act. (DW 1:7.118–19)

This unity of body and soul is significant for Eckhart's anthropology because in this life, bodily existence is inseparable from the soul uniquely created by God. Such unity is the hallmark of the Meister's anthropology, which means that a unity of act (i.e., what my eye sees and what I perceive in my mind) is never the perfection of human existence. What God is and who I am – that is our perfection, a unity of being. Let's take a moment to digest this idea (pardon the pun). Eckhart wants to stress how closely the soul unites with the body. He calls this a unity of being. The soul-body union is not like the union of action, as when the soul acts with the eye. The importance of this union of being is that it is non-dualistic. Our bodily existence is not an evil thing, opposed to a spiritual (soul) existence, which is good. Soul and body are one in being. The body is important to us both physically and spiritually. Significantly, this is similar to the kind of union that awaits us with God, which is the goal of human existence.

Practically speaking, an understanding of what it means to be human, or an anthropology based on unity of being or oneness of nature, means "peeling off" all that is not one in being, the unity of being. The focus of Eckhart's anthropology is not "how I become holy" but "how I strip away what is unholy." This is perfect peace, and as our goal, we are to run to peace – but how? Within our human nature we find breaking forth the capacity to understand and to desire, often described as the ability to know and to love. These two powers or faculties of the soul, reason and will, make us human. Eckhart says, "A Master speaks in beautiful words that never were there anything so intimate, so hidden and so strange, as the soul's uppermost where the powers of reason and will break forth" (DW 1:7.123).

Here Eckhart challenges our modern mentality once again to remind us just what an incredible gift we humans possess in our intellect and will. Our capacities to know and to love are so privileged a part of human existence that it escapes our natural understanding. Eckhart draws on the authority of St. Augustine[6] to suggest that just as the breaking forth of reason and will are ineffable, so they share in the ineffable procession of the Son from the Father. Clearly, an anthropology that regards the powers of reason and will as Godly things, beyond natural scrutiny, safeguards a sacred dimension to human existence. If we replace the term "soul" with "human person" in the following text, which concludes Sermon 7, this Godly anthropology becomes evident.

> What the soul [human person] is in its ground, of that nobody knows. What one may know of this must be supernatural, it must be by grace, and there God affects mercy. (DW 1:7.124)

While the soul remains something fundamental to the person and ought not to be reduced to "personality," we can see Eckhart's point about our humanity. Therefore, if the ground of our being is where God is acting, then we need a clearer grasp of this ground. This is what Eckhart treats as the powers of the soul.

The Three Powers of the Soul

What can be known of the essential nature, or what Eckhart called the *grunt* (ground) of reason and will, can come to us only through grace. However, knowing and willing are the keys. Here we see Eckhart's anthropology and spirituality working together. There is something at the core of human existence, but it requires us to discover it and to be enlightened by it. The soul is a hint for us, a clue in discovering the Triune God.

In Sermon 14 (DW 1:14.230-41), Eckhart demonstrates this point by associating the three powers of the soul (memory, intellect, will) with the three persons of the Trinity. This is all well and good, but he also associates these triads with three organs of the human body. Why would he go from the sublime to the mundane? At first reading, this seems odd. However, it makes perfect sense if we understand the integrity of human existence, even bodily human existence, and the hidden wonder of its ground (the soul). Eckhart writes:

> The masters and the holy ones commonly state that the soul has three powers, which make it similar to the Trinity. The first power is memory; this means an intimate hidden art, which denotes the Father. The other power is called intelligence, that is an inner presence, an admission, a wisdom. The third power is called will, a flowing forth of the Holy Spirit. We will not be satisfied with this [explanation] since it is nothing new.

> "Stand up Jerusalem and be enlightened." Another master says the soul also is dealt in three.... Anger blinds the soul and love wins the senses.... The first power is itself in the liver, the second in the heart and the third in the brain. (DW 1:14.230-31)

This harmonization of some key thinkers – Augustine on the psychological Trinity of memory, intellect and will; Galen the physician on the body's organs; and one of the most respected theologians and scientists of his day, the Dominican Albert the Great – suggests an anthropology and spirituality which sees human existence connected to the divine persons of the Trinity. Not only that, but the spiritual is physically linked to the organic members of the human body as well. Eckhart is telling us that we human beings are constituted in a similar way to God. Our bodily makeup echoes the Trinity itself. The gut of who we are is like God the Father, the heart like God the Spirit, and the mind like God the Son. These three work together. When we feel something is right in the gut, in our heart and in our head, we sense a rightness and oneness to our life and our world.

Before we go too far afield, I think a word about medieval Christian anatomy will help. By and large, the scholastics accepted the Greek appreciation of the human body as somehow consistent with the cosmos, composed of the four basic elements: earth, water, fire and air (dryness, moisture, heat and cold). Hildegard of Bingen (1098–1179), in her *Physica* and *Causae et Curae* (1150), associated these four elements with four modes of human temperament as "sanguine," "phlegmatic," "choleric" and "melancholic." Furthermore, human beings were one being in the cosmos that seemed to embrace all the ranks of creation. Some people even thought that humans possessed multiple souls: one mineral, another vegetative, another animal and another rational. However, Eckhart, like Aquinas, held to the oneness of the human soul integrating all, body and spirit. This is why the three powers of the soul reflect the same mystery of the Trinity and the biological mystery of the human animal. With this understanding, we can better see what Eckhart is doing.

The spiritual lessons found in this language of the soul bring together the first power: the Father, our memory, anger and our liver, or perhaps we might say our stomach or gut. This seems odd, but the medieval sense of human physiology, and cosmology, for that matter, were all interconnected. Recall

Thomas Aquinas on God's relation to the soul as the soul's relation to the body ("God is the spiritual life of the soul, as the soul is the life of the body" [ST II II 23, 2].). It was a common belief that the order of governance of the cosmos, seen large in creation, was repeated or reflected in the little and unseen things, and vice versa, according to their proper mode. The macrocosm (big cosmos) and the microcosm (little cosmos) reflected one another. This is why Eckhart goes on to associate the second power of the soul (now understood as the will) with the human heart. It desires the best, is satisfied only with the best, and ought to be associated with the Holy Spirit. The third power, located in the mind, unites itself to the greatest good, which is the source of all being. This is associated with the Son of God. How often we, as human beings, find our gut, our head and our heart, more than rational arguments alone, guiding us through the difficult choices in life.

Though primitive, there is a wisdom known to the "masters" and "holy ones," linking the organs of the body with the ultimate reality of God. We try to deny it, but human existence intimately integrates physical and spiritual life. In Eckhart, these three aspects of the soul (memory, intellect and will) are the primary lens for discovering the mystery of God and the inner workings of the person. The one power, memory, is hidden like our guts, but the other two, the intellect and will, play active roles in the human project, just as Christ and the Holy Spirit play active roles in salvation. These are basic elements in Eckhart's sense of the soul and human existence. Reading Eckhart rightly means that we keep this basic threefold pattern of God, the soul and our body in mind. Our ways of knowing and loving especially prepare us to receive the reality of God. This is Eckhart's concept of birthing God (*gottesgeburt*). The next section of this chapter develops Eckhart's sense of intellect and will, which is so essential to his understanding of the human person.

Deformity: A Transformative Knowing

Another crucial aspect of Eckhart's Christian anthropology is his theory of knowledge, or perhaps more correctly his transformative knowing. In talking about this concept, he fabricates a word, deiformity – our conformity to God – which he renders into German as God-birthing (*gottesgeburt*). Birthing allows something that is within to come to life. This *gottesgeburt* allows the reality of God that is already in us to come to life in us. This is not an easy step he is taking.

In our data-driven culture, we need to ask ourselves what it means for us "to know." Do we know differently when we know facts or know friends? It is a modern dilemma to realize that most of our knowing is reduced to scientific knowing (*wissen*) and that we are forced to privatize an enormous part of human knowing – familiar knowing (*kennen*). The kind of knowing which seems beyond the empirical or evident is too often dismissed in our modern world.

In a sermon, probably delivered on Trinity Sunday, our preacher offers his audience an illustration of the kind of knowing whereby we know God.[7] His scriptural text is "The earth is full of the mercy of our Lord" (Psalm 33:5). Mercy is what God effects by grace in the ground of the soul, and thus reason, or how we know the Trinity, demands an explanation. Eckhart explains this notion using St. Paul's being caught up into the third heaven and discusses three kinds of knowledge. The significance of Trinity Sunday and the human person's ability to know God at all emphasizes an anthropology that integrates humanity and divinity: deiformity. Following Augustine's interpretation of Paul's experience, Eckhart explains these "heavens" as types of knowledge present to the human person:

> The first is knowledge of creatures which one may grasp through the five senses, and all things which are present to people. In these ways, we do not know God well since they are so coarse. The second knowing is spiritual, which one may have without the object's presence, as when I know a friend a thousand miles away, whom I had previously seen. However, I must grasp him or her by likeness, which is according to the clothing, the form, place and time. This too is coarse and material knowing and according to this knowledge, one may not properly know God. One cannot know God in a place, or in time, or by appearances. The third heaven is a pure spiritual knowing where the

soul delights in all present things and bodily things. There one hears without distinct sounds, and knows without matter. There nothing is white or black or red. In this pure knowing, the soul completely knows God, as God is one in nature and threefold in persons. By this knowledge, St. John also says, "The light enlightens all who come into this world" [John 1:9]. By this, he means that knowledge that he was in at the time. One should understand these words nakedly. He [John] recognized nothing as God and everything as Godly. All those who come to this knowledge will be truly enlightened and no one else. (DW 3:61.37–39)

It is clear that a sound Christian anthropology respects the human intellect and does not reduce this capacity to reason alone. A person needs "to know" sensually and imaginatively; but one also needs to know in a manner other than the senses or the imagination. Our knowledge of God is richer than just these two types of knowing. This third kind of knowing has an impact upon human existence. Just as sense-knowing makes us perceptive (*aesthetikos*) and image-knowing makes us speculative (*theoretikos*), so too illuminative-knowing makes us.... To complete this last sentence requires much more than words can express, so we live with an ineffable gap.

For the person exploring Eckhart for the first time, he or she will wonder if Eckhart is pursuing a cult of secret knowledge – in other words, Gnosticism – as he talks about this "different kind of knowledge." He is not a Gnostic in the strict sense; but Christian mystical knowing is born of an experiential knowledge that is beyond scrutiny. Within the human core, there is a capacity to know things about which we really cannot properly talk. This becomes confusing to most 21st-century readers of Eckhart who believe that reality is what can be analyzed – if you cannot talk about it, it must not be real. For Eckhart, illuminative or transformative knowing is such knowledge beyond language that changes a person, transforms them, and brings God to birth in them. A person in love may write poems and sing songs, but knows that these words fall short of the reality that has forever changed him or her. This example only suggests the kind of knowing Eckhart invites us to. Perhaps because it defies naming we desire it even more. This desire brings us to another significant aspect of the soul: the will.

The Soul's Desires

INTRODUCING MEISTER ECKHART

Eckhart's sense of deiformity, this conformity to the reality of God, requires human effort and divine grace for the soul to thrive, thus providing the kind of integration that comes from within the soul. But how can we get a clue about what this means? To explain this reality, Eckhart uses the story of Mary Magdalene's coming to know the risen Lord at the tomb. You will recall that in this gospel story, Mary slowly came to the knowledge of the Lord's presence, transforming the person she formerly thought to be the gardener. This gospel story indicates some truths about transformative-knowing's relation to the will: what Eckhart called deiformity. He writes:

> Should the soul know when God is coming she would die of joy and if she knew when He was departing, she would die of sadness. She never knows when He comes or goes but she perfectly grasps Him when He is by her. A Master says, "His comings and goings are hidden. His presence is never hidden, for He is a light and light of its very nature illuminates." (DW 2:56.589)

As we have already seen, deiformity is a transformative knowing that the divine presence is indeed near to us, illuminating us, and revealing the divine to us. A perfect example of this can be seen in a common experience we've all probably had: waking up in a dark, unfamiliar room, perhaps in a hotel or a friend's guest room. In the darkness you think you know things. You may feel around for your slippers, or grope to get your glasses from somewhere on the nightstand. However, to your surprise, they are not there. You realize that you neglected to unpack your slippers, and before retiring you had been reading in that comfy chair across the room. You have a vague knowledge of the room, but if you attempted to act on that knowledge you might knock over a lamp, collide with a door or drawer left open, or trip on a forgotten ottoman. Therefore, you wisely reach to turn on the light and, in that instant, your knowledge of the room is illuminated, transformed.

You did not need words to explain this keen perception. By this illumination, your knowledge was transformed and you knew exactly what to do to complete your task. For Eckhart, God is that light illuminating our darkness, transforming our capacity "to know" in Godly ways so as to live Godly lives. If this is so, it seems that there must be some capacity within the human person to experience this kind of integration. Here is where the Meister turns our attention to the fundamentals of deiformity, the essentials for transformative knowing, our conforming to the reality of God, so as to "birth" God.

If we are truly looking for this deiformity, and this is a crucial "if," we have to get beyond the kind of material-mindedness of the empirical. In fact, the kind of human integration so central to Eckhart's spirituality requires an awareness of divine nearness, to "wake up" and say, "Somewhere there is a light." In our search for this deiformity, "thingly thinking" snags us, holds us back. What does this mean? I find it is one of the most common difficulties for people today. I see it most often when someone asks me to explain Eckhart in two or three sentences. If we demand that all of our thinking fit into nice neat building blocks, we will be stuck with just those blocks. Thingly thinking has to have building blocks, while deiformity knows beyond the created order of things. Furthermore, as Eckhart explains, such thingly thinking will seem sadly inadequate:

> To the soul which so seeks God every created thing should be a pain. It was a pain [for Mary] to see the angels [and not Christ]. Consequently, to the soul that would seek God, every thing is to be as a non-thing. (DW 2:56.589)

Without a doubt, this is a difficult instruction, for it is not to be seen as a rejection of the created order, as many often see it. It is rather our breaking through the created order to the divine presence (Eckhart used the word *durchbruch*), our gradual recognition of God's ever-present nearness. It is like teaching math to a young child. At first, we may need to show three balls and four balls for our young scholar to understand that this addition yields seven balls. Once he or she is able to see beyond the physical object and understand addition, the creaturely aid is no longer necessary. In fact, to have to count out every single addition would be a burden to someone who understands in this mathematical way. Similarly, we understand in a spiritual way, or non-thing way, thingly thinking is painful because it is so lacking compared to spiritual thinking or deiformity. If this is to take place in the human person, Eckhart holds that six things should be present:

> Should your soul find God she will possess six things. The first: that which was sweet to her becomes bitter. The second: that your soul becomes so cornered that she can no longer remain in herself. The third: that she longs for nothing but God. The fourth: that she is able to be consoled by no one but God. The fifth: that she could never return to the passing things. The sixth: that she will possess no inner calm until He comes to her again. (DW 2:56.589-90)

His cataloguing of these items seems to suggest that they were somewhat common wisdom for people. Other authors have spoken of similar stages that treated the pious soul's genuine human integration, requiring a core transformation from the depth of the human soul. These six things identified by Eckhart summarize Mary Magdalene's circumstances as well as our own. As pithy as these may seem, their meaning is vague. Perhaps if we take a closer look we can appreciate their deeper meaning.

According to Eckhart, Mary, seeking God, stood at the tomb weeping, looking for something she could not find. The one she sought she did not find. The corpse was gone, and instead of the body that she sought, there were two living angels. This ineffable experience of loss is what the soul desires to name but is unable to name. Here, then, are the six points. In losing Him, her life became bitter (1). The tomb was empty, crowded by created (albeit angelic) beings so that nothing remained within it (2). Mary frantically desired God, demanding to know where He is, presumably to forsake all other places and run nowhere else but there (3). Gradually Mary realizes His ever-present nearness and her longing is satisfied (4). To Mary all passing things, all created things, were seen as nothing and since they lacked God were seen as a source of pain (5). God alone satisfied her longing (6).

What might this be telling us about the soul's desires? When we know the divine nearness, our former pleasures no longer satisfy us and we long to be freed from whatever holds us back. As St. Augustine says, "Our hearts are restless until they rest in you, O Lord" (*Confessions* Bk. VI). We desire God alone. Nothing else will do. No passing things will do. Nothing but the light of divine presence will do. When we want God, everything else becomes less desirable. The things we might have desired before we were aware of God's presence in our life now no longer seem desirable. This is vital in interpreting Eckhart, yet is foreign to most readers. We find it difficult to see how we could so desire God that everything else is turned completely around, especially what normally gives us pleasure. This is a key aspect of the will, or the soul's desire for God. It is the paradox of the Gospel.

Conclusion

No modern or postmodern discourse affords us as penetrating an analysis of human integration as do the pre-modern (medieval) mystics. In Eckhart, we have one of the finest scholastic minds, a mind that sought to integrate human reason and divine revelation, addressing some of the most profound mysteries of human existence. Grasping his basic understanding of the soul, in its three powers, but especially in its knowing and desiring to be conformed to God, what he called *deiformitas*, is crucial to reading Eckhart. His anthropology has a purpose that is hidden in the very way we humans are wired. Our abilities to know and to love are what move us along toward this goal. It is in the very way that we are made as human beings that we unwrap what it is that makes us most fully human. I believe that Eckhart's concept of humanity is, for the modern reader, like the archaeologist's Rosetta stone: it enables us to decipher many of the ideas found in his mysticism. Eckhart's Christian anthropology gives to the person just starting to read Eckhart a valuable corrective lens. In having such a lens, one is better able to preserve the integrity of this complex author.

In the next chapter, I will present some of the ways Eckhart sought to help people understand the incredible reality of the human soul. His use of images to illustrate key ideas is enhanced by Fr. Bob Staes's drawings. Eckhart's use of imagery to explain the complex reality of the soul is brilliant. It is a remarkable ability of a great mind, to make what is difficult not so much easy but somehow manageable.

4

The Life of the Soul

The Soul

Eckhart was supremely aware of the soul's role in living out our human life. The life of the soul is a theme found throughout his preaching. However, unlike Thomas Aquinas's *De Anima* (*On the Soul*), there is no systematic treatment of it in Eckhart's writing. In fact, apart from his intended *Opus Tripartitum*, we have next to nothing of his that is on the scale of Aquinas's *Summa*. Yet Eckhart's thinking is not without theological depth. He gives the impression that his concerns arose from one major source, the Scriptures, and his need to understand their spiritual treasure. As with Aquinas, the revelation of Scripture was the springboard for reflection; but unlike his celebrated Dominican brother, Eckhart did not compose treatises. Rather, he responded to the circumstances he encountered. As a Master at Paris, he responded academically to the disputed questions of his time and lectured on the Scriptures in his commentaries on Genesis, Exodus and John. However, more often he responded to the preaching of the day's lessons, the life of the gospel reaching out to the life of the Christian. While his preaching is theologically demanding, he always tried to convey his meaning to the common person. To help explain his more challenging ideas, he would use illustrations or *exempla*, images or analogies.

Consequently, those looking for a more systematic treatise on the soul in Eckhart are left to hunt and gather the sources on their own. He treats the life of the soul in a number of sermons. In this chapter, I bring some of them together in a way that helps us understand Eckhart's thought on the soul. My purpose is not to collect everything he said, but to gather what will be more helpful to readers: what provides a more comprehensive understanding of the soul in Eckhart's spirituality. I believe it is important for readers even today, as my comments will show.

You may ask, "Just how does the soul work?" In one of his many sermons on the nobility of being human, Eckhart acknowledges the tensions that exist between our life here and now and our living "where life is one being" (DW 1:8.135). Simply put, this is the theme of the essential ground of our existence. Conflicts, obstacles, oppositions are all packed into living our lives, and it is the soul that grounds a person amid joys and sorrows, light and darkness. The soul helps us to root ourselves in the ground of being by our knowing things in their causes, calling us to true knowledge. It is the soul that calls us back amid the chaos of our lives. This insight is crucial in today's hectic and uncertain world. Failure to tap into this soul reality is the reason, I believe, for addiction to alcohol and drugs; for destructive behaviour; for the consumerism and materialism that weigh us down; and for the violence, terrorism and alienation that mark our world. Much criticism is rightly made of the person who arrests her or his true human development at a level of subjective autonomy, never going beyond "me" thinking.

While the people in Eckhart's day knew nothing about our contemporary critique of subjectivity, they did have their own concern about a person's proper focus in life. This is most often addressed as the inner and outer life of the soul, the spiritual and the worldly. Both aspects are important! Just as we today must see subjectivity (a healthy sense of self) and alterity (being in solidarity with others) as complementary dimensions of human existence, so too did Eckhart understand the divine, spiritual side and the created, material side.[1] This twofold quality of human life, in its process of transforming us, means that we must attend to both aspects. To help his audience understand the inner and outer life of the soul, Eckhart uses the analogy of sight. For medieval thinkers, it was the most spiritual of the five senses, since it requires no material mediation. Eckhart demonstrates the dual aspects of the soul by telling his audience of the soul's two eyes.

The Soul Has Two Eyes (from Sermon 10)

I once spoke at a cloister saying that the proper image of the soul is where nothing but God's own self is pictured forth and within. The soul has two eyes, one in-turning and the other out-turning. The inner eye is that which sees its being and takes its being from God without any middle term, which is the soul's proper work. The outer eye of the soul is that which is turned upon all created things and which senses according to images and perceptions. Whichever person is now turned in toward his or her proper self, that person is free of all changing things and is in a real castle of truth. Thus as I said, Our Lord came to the disciples on Easter through closed doors, just as He comes to every person who is free of all otherness and created-ness. In such a person God does not "come" for God is already essentially there. (DW 1:10.165)

This image of the soul's two eyes is a powerful yet confusing one. The two eyes represent ways of knowing: one eye knows perceptively, the other eye knows essentially. That is, part of us knows things through what our senses perceive, while another part of who we are knows things not by the external trappings but in the thing itself, its essential reality. When we come to know God with both eyes, we know the full vision of God. It is an awesome proposition, knowing God essentially. This dual aspect of knowing can be seen as the split between the empirical realm and the spiritual realm. In one realm, we know by things, facts, ideas, equations; in the other, we know by nothing, a non-mediated or immediate perception of truth. The modern dilemma is that we look for truth in only one realm: the empirical. Our outward eye demands scientific proof, not seeing the essential ground, while our inward eye sees by a gut perception, a hidden truth. In fact, both types of knowing in the soul bring us to a more perfect knowledge.[2]

For Eckhart, a Christian anthropology, or Christian sense of who we are, is not to be found in the clear and distinct ideas of Cartesian rationalism. This overemphasizes subjective knowledge as the ground for one's existence. Eckhart, rather, makes existence the ground for knowing. Simply "to be" means that both difference (how things are not the same) and otherness (how other people are not me) are present. Our existence embraces both the physical and material realities of our life, but more importantly, it embraces everything other than that. We exist according to creaturely things, but essentially, in the ground of being, all differences dissolve. The doors we lock to otherness or createdness do not define the Easter experience, as Eckhart presents it. It is not about denying creation, but about discovering something already present, God's ever-present nearness. This type of knowing is a threat to the kind of superficial knowing that modern consumerist society demands. Eckhart is telling us that we must learn to see with both eyes of the soul.

With this image of the two eyes, we have an illustration of how we are to know things, and it is a common theme in Eckhart's preaching. He further instructs us about each eye through *exempla* that treat the inner and outer life of the soul. In the following sections, we will look at these two realities – the inner and the outer life of the soul – as found in various sermons.

The Inner Life

The eye-that-looks-within is perhaps the more intriguing notion, but its capacity to see the essence of things without words is perhaps the most foreign to readers. The *exempla*, taken from three sermons and presented below, lend themselves to our better appreciating the inner life. They illustrate the inner reality moving outward, the mysterious source at work in the soul, its desire for truth and goodness, and its transcendence of the here and now. In the first, Eckhart uses the image of our taking God clothed or naked. The image is both an amusing and an engaging way to present the eye of inner knowing.

God, Naked or Clothed? (from Sermon 2)

A pagan Master said: The soul, which loves God, takes God under the veil of the Good – still all these [other sources] about which I have spoken have been pagan masters who were familiar with a natural light. I have yet to come to the words of the holy Masters who were familiar with a much higher light. One says, "The soul, which loves God, takes God under the veil of the Good. [But the soul which knows God] seeks God without this veil of the Good and takes God na-

THE LIFE OF THE SOUL

ked where he is disrobed of Goodness and Beingness and from all labels."

I said in the school [at Paris] that intellect was nobler than the will and still both belong to this [higher] light. A Master in one of the other schools [very likely Master Gonsalvo] said that the will was really nobler than reason since the will takes things as they are in themselves and the intellect takes things as they are in the intellect. It is true that an eye is nobler in itself than is the [image of] an eye that has been drawn on a wall. However, I say that intellect is nobler than will since will takes God under the garments of the Good. Intellect takes God naked, as He is unclothed of the Good or Being. Good is a garment under which God is concealed and the will [merely] takes God as the garments of the Good. In fact, if the Good were not in God my will would not desire Him. Anyone who would dress a king in grey on the day he is crowned would not have clothed him well. Therefore, I do not become blessed because God is Good. I will never beseech my God to make me blessed by His Goodness since He would never do such a thing. Consequently, I am only blessed since God is intellectual and I know this. (DW 1:2.152–53)

The fact that the human soul possesses two faculties – reason and will – makes us distinctively human. "Intellect," since the Enlightenment, has taken on rationalistic meanings. Today, to be labelled an "intellectual" is very often a put-down. It says the person is too much in their head and out of touch with the real world. Intellect, to most people, equals cerebral, impractical and boring. These meanings are absent from Eckhart's sense of intellect, or the soul that knows God. For lack of a better word, we still use "intellect" to translate something that is fuller and richer in meaning. Intellect, here, carries more a sense of the spiritual than we are used to assigning to it. For Eckhart, the intellectual power enables us to break beyond the good desires of our will. Because of our intellect, we seek even in these good things something more, which is the ground of goodness – the naked reality of God.

It is the inner living of the soul that pushes us beyond the apparent, to the nobler realities. Here is where we discover our Godly ground, which brings about deiformity. This conformity to God is essential to the inner life of the soul as it strives for blessedness. We find true deiformity, taking God naked, in our inwardly knowing the Truth of reality. It is "a stripping away" of all that keeps us from this pure Truth. It is a nakedness beyond even the manifold goods of genuine human existence.

This inner eye, or inner life of the soul, will not be satisfied with anything less than God, no matter how good the good thing is. Ultimately, we are ordered to the eternal, and our journey means that we move beyond the particularity of created good. In the next sermon (Sermon 42), we see how Eckhart promotes our movement beyond the temporal and spatial to the eternal.

Beyond Here and Now (from Sermon 42)

> The soul has two powers that are independent of the body. They are intellect and will, operating beyond time. Oh if only the soul's eyes were opened so that our imagination could clearly gaze upon this Truth! Do you realize that such a person could easily abandon everything as if they were but a grain or a pea or nothing at all? Indeed, by my soul [I swear] that to such a person all things would be as nothing! Now there are some people who give up things out of a sense of love and dearly miss the things they've given up. However [the kind of] person [that I mean], one who knows that even if he or she abandons self and all things in

THE LIFE OF THE SOUL

Truth they are nothing, such a person who so lives truly possesses all things.

There is a power in the soul to which all things are equally sweet. Indeed all the worst and all the best are the same to this power, which grasps things beyond "here" and "now." "Now," that is time and "here," that is place, the place wherein I now stand. In addition, were I to go out of myself and become completely empty then the Father would perfectly birth his only-begotten Son in my spirit [if] my spirit [would] bear him back. Yes, by God's Truth, were my soul as ready as the soul of our Lord Jesus Christ then truly the Father would work in me as perfectly as [He does] in His only begotten Son, no less, for God loves me with the same love with which He loves himself. St. John says, "In the beginning was the Word, and the Word was with God and the Word was God" (Jn. 1:1). Now [in order] to hear this Word in the Father, where all is perfectly still, a person must be perfectly still and free from all images and concepts. A person should keep oneself so true to God that in all things nothing could delight or darken. One should take all things in God as they are there [in God]. (DW 2:42.305–7)

Here we see that for Eckhart, the soul's powers of intellect and will are the inner realities by which we come to transcend even time and space. Knowledge of this truth is crucial, and is the key to our intellect's "seeing" this. It seems so simple a truth to Eckhart, yet it is to that truth that we are most frequently blind. How often do we make our judgment on superficial realities? It seems to be the plague of our time. Image is everything. We buy the package and not the product. Time and space are created categories (part of the packaging) with which we humans are most at home, literally standing in their midst. "What a difference a day makes," as the saying goes. If we took the time to look at reality, if we changed our perspective and looked at life from another place, what a difference it would make. The inner life of the soul is about transcending these limitations. Imagine how you would view life if it were not confined by temporal and spatial limitations. When and where become meaningless. Distinctions like before and after, here and there, melt away. God, who is beyond time and place, has no now and then, no here and there. God is always and everywhere. In a certain sense, Eckhart anticipates an Einsteinian universe with a spiritual theory of relativity that redefines our thinking about life. Rather than thinking of God's action in terms of our temporal and spatial situation, with its relative sense of God, we must go beyond these limits by a perfect emptying. If we could or would attain such perfection, the divine action that is grace could and would act freely in us. This is an amazing insight and brings Eckhart to the unorthodox-sounding notion that a person freed of spatial-temporal limitations would give birth to God in the world just as God was born in Christ. This is, I think, theoretically possible for Eckhart's thinking, but even he realizes that the more important and more realistic point is that we make a start. We find this starting point in our becoming still, in transcending time and place. It is in this inner stillness that we possess all created things, both spatial and temporal. In such stillness, we discover something of grace in us, which he describes as the light of the soul. We discover this stillness by letting go of all that is not God, what Eckhart calls *gelâzenheit* (letting-go-ness).

A Light in the Soul (from Sermon 48)

Again, we are allowing Eckhart to teach us about the incredible inner life of the soul. This is something very different for most modern readers, for whom programming their cell phone or solving computer problems can be a challenge. This is why the *exempla* play a valuable role in helping us grasp his message. It is in this next image, of the light or spark in the soul (*funklein*), that many a new reader has become lost. If we bear in mind that it pertains to an inner knowing proper to the soul, we will see that the image is about divine immanence and not self-divinization; it is about discovering that God is within us, but we are not God!

> I have occasionally spoken about a light in the soul that
> is uncreated and uncreatable. This light I frequently
> treat in my preaching and this very light grasps God
> without mediation or coverings but naked, as God is
> in himself. That is, it grasps God as the efficaciousness
> of inner birthing. Indeed I may truly state that by this
> light I am united with God more than I am united to
> any power, with this light I am truly one. You should
> know [for a fact] that this light is no nobler in the
> being of my soul than the lowest powers or the high-
> est ones like hearing or seeing or any other power by
> which hunger or thirst, cold or heat might effect us.
> And that is the debt, being is indivisible. Therefore,
> if one understands these powers essentially [in terms
> of indivisible being], then they are all one and equally
> noble, but if one understands them in their works, then
> one power is much more noble and much higher than
> the others.
>
> Consequently, I say that when a person turns from the
> [selfish-] self and from all creaturely things – as much as
> one is able to do this – then that is how much you will
> be united and made holy in the spark of the soul where
> time and place never disturb. This spark is contrary to
> all created things and it desires nothing but God naked,
> as God is in Himself. It is not enough [to desire God]
> just as the Father or just as the Son or just as the Holy
> Spirit, or even [to desire] the three Persons if each is
> taken in its own distinct properties. I say truly that this

117

light is not even satisfied with the oneness of the divine nature's fruits. I will say still more, which is even more amazing, I say by goodly Truth, by the eternal Truth and the never ending Truth that this very same light is not [even] satisfied by the indivisible changeless divine essence which neither gives nor takes. Moreover, it wants to know from whence this essence comes, it wants the indivisible ground in the silent desert where no distinctions of Father or Son, or Holy Spirit ever set foot, in the inmost where it is never [completely] at home. There this light is satisfied and there it is more inner than it is in itself. There your ground is one indivisible stillness and your inner self is unmoved and from this immovability are all things moved and all things commence to live, and your spiritual lives are in the inner self. (DW 2:48.418–21)

This "light" of the soul, or the *funklein (vunkelein)*, shares in a complex neo-Platonic tradition on the divine spark of the soul, the *scintilla animae*. In fact, any reader needs to be careful not to allow Eckhart's orthodox meaning to slip into some unorthodox neo-Platonist interpretations.[3] His Christian understanding of the soul suggests something of the Divine indwelling and the soul's (human person's) ultimate goal (*telos*). According to Eckhart, the inner life is a coming to this essential reality, the ever-present divine nearness, out of which all else is ordered. It is this still point that moves all things, and from this still point we live our spiritual lives inside out, grounded in the Creator but lived amid the creatures.

It is from this essential ground that we live our lives, and without this foundation the outer life, the active life, is not truly lived. Eckhart holds up to his listeners the twofold life of the soul and, as we have seen, he illustrates this with the image of two eyes. The inner-looking eye comes to know the essential reality of God and is able to see beyond the limits of here and now. Such an inner vision is something truly remarkable in a person. It guides and directs everything he or she does. It is important that Eckhart uses the image of two eyes, for both eyes are necessary in order to see rightly, and the loss of one eye is a privation. As with normal sight, the loss of vision in one eye takes away something provided by both eyes together: that is, the perception of depth, the distance of an object. Consequently, the inner life of the soul, while it is the important ground, is matched by the outer life of the soul, the eye that looks outward. We'll examine the outer life next.

The Outer Life

By outer life, Eckhart means the active, moral life. Sometimes people have the impression that mystics are concerned only about prayer and inner peace, a kind of spiritual escapism. We have seen in Part I how Eckhart's life was anything but an escape from the commerce of his day. So how did he convey this active life to his audience?

A Life of Virtue (from Sermon 32)

The inner life is the all-important principle for Christian living, but it must be a life that moves out to the world, a life lived virtuously. The sermons selected here help us to see the importance Eckhart places on our engaging the world. It is important to distinguish the inner oneness, which we have seen to be found in the life of the soul, from the multiplicity of creation, so we can live our present lives rooted in the mystery of the Trinity. Yet, we must manifest, or bring to fruition, the full flowering of this life in today's world. This is achieved in a life of virtue.

> Saint Augustine said that the soul is so noble and so superiorly created above all creatures that no perishable thing could, even from the earliest days [of creation], speak to the soul or act upon it without the intervention of distinct [means. These means] are the eye and ear and the [other] five senses. They are the avenue by which the soul goes out into the world and by these avenues the world is brought back into the soul. A Master said, "The powers of the soul should run back to the soul laden with abundant fruits." [Just] as it goes out so it must bring something back. Therefore one should especially heed the eyes and what they bring [into the soul] lest the soul become corrupted. I am sure that whatever a good person sees this will be to his or her advantage. If [the good person] sees sin, he thanks God for having been safeguarded from it and prays [for the person in sin] to return to God. If [the

good person] sees the good, she delights in its coming to fruition in the person.

This "seeing" should be twofold: one is to eschew what would be harmful and [the other is to] capitalize from one's shortcomings. I have also said that many [people] fast and keep vigil and do great deeds but do not improve [their lives] or mend [their ways] or circumstances, wherein true perfection lies. They deceive themselves and are the devil's scorn. A man had a porcupine by which he [became] rich. He lived near the sea and when the porcupine sensed from whence the wind would blow, it curled up its bristles and turned its back toward that direction. So the man went to the coastal town and asked them, "What would you give me if I were to tell you from which direction the wind [will be] blowing?" He thus sold the wind and became rich by [doing] this. So too a person will become rich in virtues if he or she can tell what are his or her real imperfections and by this become better, or what are his or her temptations in order to overcome them. (DW 2:32.137–40)

For Eckhart, the life of the soul necessarily involves commerce with the real world. We are sensual beings and, in keeping with what Thomas Aquinas taught, what comes into our soul must come via the senses. Hearing, but especially seeing, relays the outside world in a non-corporeal way, by sound and sight. The other senses depend on coarser, mediated methods, so it is particularly important that we be careful with what we hear and see. We must capitalize on this commerce between the soul and the world, and the world back to the soul. To a person who looks to find what is the good, the world is not bad, even in the midst of evil. Should people find themselves beset by evil or sin, they must try to figure out how to turn this to their gain. The life of virtue is built through good acts, which become habitual. If we are ignorant of our actions, our choices, our circumstances, we fail to capitalize, to grow rich even from our shortcomings. The sensual life is meant to go out to the world, but must return to the soul laden with the fruits of its forays. In doing this, a person grows rich in the life of virtue. But who is doing this: God or me?

One and Yet Not One (from Sermon 72)

Certainly we need to protect against a kind of overemphasis on works, as though what we do is the important thing. Rather, our actions, our living the virtuous life, should proceed from the inner life. When this happens, our actions remain virtuous, moving from the inner life of the soul out to the world. For Eckhart, this is not unlike the Son's procession from the Father in the Incarnation.

A Master says, "The soul cannot know itself apart from images but angels know themselves and God without images." He means to tell us that God gives himself most supremely to the soul, without [the need of] any images and likenesses.

"He went up the mountain and was transfigured before them" [Mt. 17:2]. The soul should be transfigured [or re-imaged] and formed in the image and recast in that image which is the Son of God. The soul is imaged according to God, but a Master says that the Son is the Image of God and the soul is imaged according to the Image. So I say that the Son is the image of God beyond images. He is the image of the hidden Godhead. The Son is the Image of God and there the soul is imaged in the manner the Son images. Just as the Son takes [his proper image] there, so too the soul takes [her proper image]. Consequently, there, [where] the Son is the out-flowing of the Father, the soul is not dependant [on likeness since] she is beyond image. Fire and heat are one and yet far from one. The taste and colour of the apple are one and yet far from one. The mouth takes the flavour, which the eye is not capable of doing; [while] the eye takes the colour in a manner that the mouth cannot. The eye must have light while the flavour is [still] perfect in the dark. The soul knows not why it is one, this is beyond image. (DW 3:72.243–46)

This complicated question on the soul's self-knowledge that takes place beyond conceptualization may seem more appropriate to the inner life. However, this self-knowing is essential to the outer life of the soul. For Eckhart, the soul is very close to God – perhaps even too close, from a theological point of view. Nevertheless, this means that the soul must be able to know itself without mediating likenesses. Consequently, the soul is transfigured in the image of God.

So, how is it possible, if Jesus is the Image of God, for the soul also to be the image of God? Because it is both our outer life in Christ as well as our inner life of the soul that know the out-flowing of the Godhead. Our soul and Christ are one, yet they are not the same. The soul's reception of this divine out-flowing is distinct according to its capacities, for Christ has this out-flowing in a manner most fitting to the incarnate Image of God. Just as an apple is received by both the eye and the mouth, so too divine out-flowing is received by both the soul and Christ, each one according to its own unique capacities. In living our lives, we are transfigured by the Image of the Son so that in the inner life of the soul we might come to know our oneness with God.

As we saw in the previous sermon (32), our outer life is integrally related to the inner life, and the virtuous life is meant to edify the soul. In this sermon, Sermon 72, we see that our lives are transfigured in Christ. In this way, we understand the soul's oneness both in Christ and in the soul's out-flowing from the Godhead. The soul really is the image of God, but in a manner proper to our human capacities. Just as a cloth sack is suited to hold things that need to breathe, or a glass jug is suited to hold a pint of water, so too we as human beings are suited to things in a particular way. The Son is truly the image of God's hiddenness in a manner different from the human soul, and far superior. God, Christ and the soul are one, yet not one, just as the colour and sweetness of the apple are one, yet not one. The living of our outer life is one, yet not one. We will see this in the next sermon, which uses the illustration of a root.

Living from an Inner Root (from Pfeiffer 61)[4]

In this image, we see how the active and contemplative lives, or the outer and inner lives, are ordered. If you are unfamiliar with Eckhart, this is a valuable corrective for those who would accuse all mystics of being out of touch with the world. It also shows the kind of groundedness which contemplation gives to action.

> I say concerning God's freedom that it yields no nature save one. God starts with the Son, and the Son is another than the Father who is power, and from them twain there blossoms forth the Holy Ghost. Our philosophers teach that the sun draws the flowers out of the roots through the stem, timelessly well-nigh and too subtly for any eye to follow. The soul, which has no nature in her ground, the ground of love, where she is love, emerges from this nature where she is stored in God. Whatever enters this being has much the same being. At the coming of the bride he devotes himself to her and works with all his might within his ground, in his innermost, where naught exists, where activity stops altogether. The tree of the Godhead grows in this ground and the Holy Ghost sprouts from its root. The flower that blossoms, love, is the Holy Ghost. In this Holy Ghost the soul flowers with the Father and

the Son, and on this flower there rests and reposes the Spirit of the Lord. He could not repose had he not rested first upon the Spirit. The Father and the Son rest on the Spirit, and the Spirit reposes upon them as on its cause. What is rest? St. Augustine says, rest is complete lack of motion: body and soul bereft of their own nature. One philosopher says, God's idio-syncrasy is immutability. That is, all creatures. Man as transcending motion. *Jesse* means a fire and a burn-ing; it signifies the ground of divine love and also the ground of the soul. Out of this ground the rod grows, i.e. in the purest and highest; it shoots up out of this virgin soil at the breaking forth of the Son. Upon the rod opens a flower, the flower of the Holy Ghost. We beseech the Lord our God that we may rest in him and he in us to his glory. (Evans, 154)

In this sermon, we see that the outer life, our virtuous life, one that is born of a free will or in fact of God's freedom, is parallel to the divine life. Just as the life of the Trinity is both repose and flowering, the soul can participate in this repose and flowering, but we must live from this root.

Eckhart's Scriptural inspiration is Isaiah 11:1, the shoot coming forth from the root of Jesse. The soul, in us, shares in the divine life from the ground of repose or perfect rest; but at the same time, a shoot must sprout forth. That sprout of love must also flower with the fruit of the Holy Spirit. Just as this flowering happens in the Godhead, so too it takes place in us, in a manner proper to our nature. While the sermon's transla-tion becomes confusing in its notion of divine immutability, the central point is not immobility (a kind of spiritual quiet-ism) but rising above the mobility, the transience of life. The root from the ground of repose must shoot forth and flower; this is the glory of God.

Clearly, these are complicated notions, but Eckhart did not give up trying to find ways of getting his ideas across. As human beings, we find images very helpful. Eckhart knew this. In the next section of this chapter, I will present three *exempla* or illustrations wherein Eckhart speaks of God's presence in the soul.

God and the Soul: Three Images of Grace

The task of conveying the reality of grace, of God's divine action in the person, is extremely complex. Any reader of Eckhart needs to keep in mind the concept of divine action and humankind's collaboration in that action. It is the question of grace, God's action and our human freedom in that action. How we preserve God's transcendence and our human freedom has haunted theologians from Augustine on through Thomas Aquinas, Martin Luther, Francisco Suarez, Domingo Bañez, Karl Rahner and Edward Schillebeeckx. In this section, we will examine three illustrations or *exempla* from Eckhart's preaching that help to explain how God enters into the human person without violating human nature or lessening the divine Godhead. These *exempla* articulate an incredibly rich theological and spiritual truth, even if we fall short in how we name it.

A Mirror (from Pfeiffer 56)

The analogy of the mirror and the soul is a common one among medieval spiritual writers such as Bernard of Clairvaux and Marguerite of Porette, a contemporary of Eckhart's whose infamous *Mirror of Simple Souls* led to her condemnation. The "Mirror of the Prince" (*speculum Regis*), a class of medieval books offering counsel to the ruling classes, may have been Marguerite's inspiration. Regardless, the "mirror" metaphor holds properties conducive to explaining the spiritual life. The mirror provides a visual image (itself non-corporeal) of one's self so as to see the self. This reflective property and the question of its source is what Eckhart uses in his analogy to treat the inner person's appreciation of the created world.

> To return to my inner and outer man, I see the lilies in the field, their gaiety, their colour, all their leaves. But I do not see their fragrance. Why? Because what I give out is in me. What I am to say is in me and I speak it forth of me. My outward man relishes creatures as creatures, as wine and bread and meat. But my inner man relishes things not as creature but as the gift of God. And again to my innermost man they savour not of God's gift but of ever and aye. I take a bowl of water and place a mirror in it and set it in the sun. The sun sends forth his light-rays both from his disc and also from the bottom of the bowl, suffering thereby no diminution. The reflection of the mirror in the sun is in the sun. The sun and it are thus what it is. And so with God. God is in the soul with his nature, his essence and his Godhood, but he is not on that account the soul. The soul's reflection is in God. God and she are thus what she is. There God is all creatures. There God's utterance is God. (Evans, 143)

Eckhart is not a mystic who condemns the created world. Clearly, our outer person "relishes" the goods of creation, but it is the inner person that comes to know these created things as they reflect or reveal God. However, even more than this, the inner person, attuned to the divine "rays," reflects the divine nature. This is characteristic of Eckhart's kind of negative theology, stripping away what is not God. For Eckhart, God is in the soul but is not the same as the soul. What our soul reflects, in this case, is truly in God, yet with no diminishment of the divine essence. This is a complex metaphysical concept that Eckhart packages in the *exemplum* of the mirror in water. There is an inner reality, capable of reflecting the divine nature that is not apparent, for it is beneath the surface, but it must be placed in relation to the "God-rays." In this relation, the soul is in God and God is in the soul, respecting the proper nature of each. Just as the sun is in the mirror but is not the mirror and the mirror manifests the sun but is not the sun, God is both immanent and transcendent. This twofold reality is critical to our understanding Eckhart's mysticism. We need to preserve the tension between God's subjective reality in our lives yet not deny God's absolute otherness beyond us.

A Flask (from Sermon 59)

If the reader of Eckhart should have any doubts about his orthodox use of immanence and transcendence, it is further presented in the *exemplum* of the flask. It may be valuable to repeat the distinction we saw earlier between a unity of act (e.g., what my eye sees and what I perceive in my mind) and a unity of being (e.g., what I eat and its unity with my body). If this is unclear, refer to "A Basic Understanding of the Soul" in Chapter 3 of this book. It is this unity of being – God's immanence and transcendence – that the flask *exemplum* illustrates.

> Now He [Christ] says: "The Father and I are One" – the soul in God and God in the soul. The water is inside of the flask thus [we say it] contains the water within it, but the water is not truly in the flask and the flask is not truly in the water. However, the soul is definitely one with God so that the one without the other would be incomprehensible. One can understand heat even without the fire and the rays without the sun, but God is unable to understand Himself without the soul, nor the soul without God, so completely one are they. (DW 2:59.631–32)

Again, we see Eckhart treating this question of how to help understand the truth of divine union with the soul and still preserve the proper distinction, or absolute transcendence of God, while safeguarding human freedom. Being, in God, is something other than physically "containing." Still, there is a true unity. This unity for Eckhart is crucial: everyone, by virtue of their soul, is in fact one with God. The logical consequence of this unity is that even if we abandon God, God remains ever one with us. This is an amazing truth about God and is inexhaustible in its scope. No matter how vile, evil or Godless a person seems to be, he or she is never without God. On the part of God, divine union is not an on-again, off-again thing, even though we might think in these terms: that is incomprehensible to God. We must be careful not to presume that what is intellectually distinguishable (heat from fire, rays from sun, soul from God) is possible when it comes to God.

A Tub (from Sermon 64)

As in the previous sermon (59), Eckhart stresses the unique reality of the soul's relation to God. So often when we say that two things are one – for example, in marriage, when we say the two become one – we mean that they are united. Being united and being one are different things. We can speak of things that are united as being one, yet they remain distinguishable in this unity, as we see in the tub *exemplum*.

The text says: the soul is one with God and not united. This indicates a similitude. [If] one fills a [wooden] tub with water, the water is united with the vat but not one [with the tub] since where there is water there is no wood, and where there is wood there is no water. Now take the wood and throw it in the middle of the sea. Still the wood is only united and not one. [But] it is not so with the soul which is one with God and not united. Wherever God is, there is the soul and where the soul is there is God. (DW 3:64.86)

Spiritual unity is different. We understand a bit of this in the phrase "they were all of one mind." Such a unity defies distinction. When the soul is one with God, and this is already a very important qualification, there is no distinction. This, I believe, is the key to Eckhart's mysticism. We are not guaranteed oneness with God by virtue of our soul, for our freedoms can thwart the soul's becoming one by not co-operating with grace. However, when the soul is one with God, all distinction between soul and God ceases, for they are not united but are in fact one: they are intellectually indistinguishable. Clearly, such a teaching is theologically possible, but in this life it is difficult in its ambiguity.

Living from an Inner Ground

It ought to be apparent that Eckhart's concept of the soul is a crucial one to understand if we want to read him rightly. The life of the soul, or what we might call human flourishing, necessarily begins from an inner ground where we are attentive to the divine. However, this contemplative stance must lead to commerce with the world. In fact, the life of virtue is essential to this flowering, but must be rooted within. It is in the life of the soul that the human venture encounters its fullest flourishing by its openness to the divine will. This unity manifests God.

So often people just starting to read Eckhart might naively think that this soul concept is about the subjective ego. They think that it is all about them, but this is absurd. For example, a true friendship can never be just about one person. This belief reduces the rich meaning of a true friendship to just one-half of that friendship. Imagine not knowing a friend's likes and dislikes, hopes and fears, desires and dreams. If we have friends only because they think like us, act the way we want them to act, agree with everything we say and do, then something is wrong. Such a situation is ridiculous. To try to understand a friendship without the otherness of the friend is to miss the point. The same is true in understanding Eckhart. What is worse, an egotistical understanding of the soul cheapens the richness of Eckhart's insight into human existence. We are most truly who we are as humans because of our relationship, our friendship with God.

What I have done in these first four chapters has been to prepare you to read Meister Eckhart in a way that respects his program. As we saw, the reality of his life and the importance of his understanding of the soul are both crucial concepts for a person living today who wants to enter into Eckhart's spiritually rich sense of things. The *exempla* or illustrations he used further support this approach. We need to imagine beyond the limits of our present-day set of thingly categories. The *exempla* allow our minds to be illumined by a transformative knowing. Just as the click of a light switch can illumine a dark and unfamiliar room, Eckhart's *exempla* "click" on our imaginations so we can see the world in a new way, and in that knowledge live rightly. In the next chapter, I present additional *exempla*, or illustrations, drawn from the Meister's preaching that instruct us in this life of the soul, our Christian anthropology. This section is offered for meditation and reflection. If you allow these *exempla* to unfold, they will enrich your grasp of Eckhart and help you to understand this mystic's message on the soul, the flourishing of the human venture.

PART III

The Exempla

In the first and second parts of this book I presented a condensed treatment of Eckhart's life and understanding of the soul. This concept in Eckhart is crucial in reading his mysticism because it addresses the very nature of human existence. Both Eckhart's life and his sense of human flourishing are essential tools for a person interested in understanding this fourteenth-century theologian, preacher and mystic. In Part II we began to see how this preacher's use of illustrations, or *exempla*, helped to explain some important aspects of his thought. It is remarkable that a gifted scholar of Paris, versed in the categories of scholastic thought, was able to preach many of these same ideas to people who had never studied philosophy. His use of these *exempla* remains a timeless feature that enables even today's beginners to grasp something of his penetrating mind.

In his preaching, Eckhart's use of visual imagery was not graphic but auditory. He used both the power of his words and the imagination of his audience. Certainly the churches in which he preached had their share of religious art. But Eckhart's ideas needed some other help if his non-university hearers were to understand. The use of *exempla* was common among preachers; Jesus' parables are a worthy demonstration of their capacity to instruct the believer. *Exempla*, in a sense, brought the ideas home to a person. Concepts like "forgiveness" are made real in the story of the prodigal son; "moral character" in the story of the sower and the seed; "God's justice" in the story of the rich man and Lazarus. They provide us with a vivid and memorable image whose deeper meaning later begins to surface. Such *exempla* or illustrations are common in Eckhart's preaching. In the same way they helped people to understand in his day, they can help us today.

However, there is one major difference between Eckhart's times and our own, and this deserves special note. Whereas Eckhart spoke to an audience, to listeners, we today are largely spectators, viewers. The visual image is our chief modern medium. Even very primitive pictures help us get the ideas that our ears are hearing. This is why it is so important to include artwork in this book. The amazing thing about *exempla* is that they want us to draw them out: first in our imagination, then in a more graphic way. These images offer us the reverse task: to enter back into the more imaginative parts of our minds and explore these *exempla* more deeply.

In Chapter 5, I offer the reader a series of illustrations extracted from the texts of Eckhart's sermons. As a respected preacher and teacher, Eckhart was interested in providing his listeners with analogies. He wanted to give these men and women of noble families and of the growing merchant class images that would help them understand some aspects of the spiritual life, as illustrated in their daily lives. The selections in this chapter are a sample of his *exempla*, illustrations or illuminations, and are just segments of the larger sermon. Here I invite you to engage these *exempla* as they explain key spiritual insights found in Eckhart. I provide the illustration's context in the sermon so you can appreciate the biblical inspiration. For each sermon I begin with the liturgical text that inspired this preacher's sermon. This is followed by Eckhart's translation of what would have been read to the people in Latin, since his translation often takes liberties with the Latin. Then I give a brief sense of what the entire sermon aims to do. I present the *exemplum* itself and invite you to reflect on its meaning, asking that you take time to digest his ideas. Reflection is a lost art; it requires a contemplative sense to allow us to discover our true self. Imagine looking into the agitated surface of a pool of water; we see nothing but jagged glimpses. We must let the waters settle so we can see ourself reflected. Reflection is the stilling of the waters in our lives so we can catch sight of our true self.

Bob Staes's art helps us reflect by providing what are known as "uncials," the medieval custom of embellishing the first letter of a text with the images that the text addresses. Taken as a whole – the context, the *exemplum*, the uncial and my own comments on the text – they provide a source for personal prayer and reflection, time taken to encounter the truest ground of one's self. Whereas the previous two sections were instructional, I hope that you enter Part III differently, since it is meant to be more formative, speaking to your very soul. At the very least, I hope Part III invites you to a more reflective, contemplative reading of Eckhart.

5

Ten Illustrations for Personal Reflection

The value of this chapter is what I think Eckhart meant the *exempla* to be: the hearer's own pondering on the illustration's meaning. Consequently, I encourage the reader to use these ten *exempla* as starting points for meditating on the concept Eckhart is presenting. This invites us to contemplate the deeper meaning in these simple illustrations. Meister Eckhart knew well the power of images, the spiritual *phantasmata* that the mind is able to see, even when the object is nowhere to be seen. As a preacher and teacher he knew that people need such images to help them understand. The use of these *exempla* was a common practice. Images stay with us and allow us to unfold their meaning. In treating the spiritual life, Eckhart was faced with conveying important theological concepts. Metaphysics is not an easy thing to explain. Eckhart's use of images to illustrate his ideas provides a masterful way to understand him.

Eckhart's spirituality is born of some fundamental ideas about God's relationship to us, our relationship to God, how we live our life and our ultimate destiny. The following illustrations convey these themes and invite the reader to enter Eckhart's spirituality through these images. They provide an illustrated introduction that will enrich one's further study of "the man from whom God hid nothing," as his pupil Johannes Tauler called him.

I. (from Sermon 10)

Wine in the Cellar

Sermon Text: Sirach 44:17, which Eckhart translates as "He was found just within, in his days, he had well pleased God in his days."

In this sermon, which was probably preached July 31 on the feast of St. Germanus (now celebrated July 25), who was Bishop of Paris, Eckhart develops the importance of the inner life as ground for true justice.

The person who now knows all as God knows is a God-knowing person. This person takes God in God's uniqueness of self, in God's oneness of self, God's presence of self, and in God's trueness of self. This person is truly just. But the person, who is not at home with inward things, is a person that does not know what God is. It [would be] like a person who has wine in their cellar but hasn't tasted it or [even] examined it. Such a person doesn't know if this wine is good [or not]. So it is with people who live unreflectively. They know nothing about God, and yet they think and presume to be living. Such knowledge is not of God. A person must possess a pure and clear knowing of divine truth. For any person with the right intention, all his or her actions are intentionally inaugurated by God and the effect[ive cause] of their intentions is God Himself.

The consummation of [our] pure divine nature is in the Divine Nature of God's self. (DW 1:10.164)

Reflection

- How do you come to know God?
- What impact does this knowledge have in your life?

Commentary

This illustration addresses the mystery of the inner life where grace works in us according to our human nature. Many people are ignorant of this inner life of grace, which ultimately brings us to blessedness. We can deceive ourselves into believing that we understand who we are and the meaning of our lives. Many good people understand and can analyze their motives, or their personality types and psychological profiles, without ever entering the inner cellar to taste the wine of Godly knowing. What person wouldn't want to go into their cellar in order to taste the vintage wine? Yet our world is full of sad and lonely people who never look within. It is from this inner depth that we taste the meaning of divine nature; this inaugurates our moral living.

II. (from Sermon 12)

Sailing with Half a Wind

Sermon Text: Sirach 24:30 [NRSV 24:22], which Eckhart translates as "Whoever hears me will not be ashamed."

Essentially, this sermon is on obedience, our truly hearing

God, and the obstacles to this obedience. Hearing the Word of God requires self-surrender, which allows true love. Ultimately this means loving without a multiplicity of things getting in the way. How do we convey the necessity of this kind of simple love, yet acknowledge the limits of the human heart?

> Have [genuine] love for your self and so you will have love for all people as for your self. While your love for any single person remains less than [your love] for your self, you really don't love your self. You must love all people as you do your self, all people in one person, and that person is [both] God and man. Thus a person is Just who [both] loves self and loves all people as self. To such a person all is right. Now some people say, "I have greater love for my friend who is good to me than I have for other people." Such [an attitude] is unjust and imperfect. Even so, one must tolerate it, [just] as some people travel the seas [catching] only half the wind and still they make it across. These are the people who love one person more than another, which is [quite] natural. If I had right love, [loving] as I love self, then whatever happens, be it joy or sorrow, life or death, it happens in me as in my friend and that truly is right friendship. (DW 1:12.195)

Reflection

- How would you explain genuine love?
- Why is genuine love for your self essential in order to love others?

Commentary

Love of neighbour, but especially love of our enemies, is a difficult task in the spiritual life that hasn't changed since the days of Eckhart. In this illustration, the Meister shifts the focus for testing this love from an external consequence to the internal principle of such love, which is the capacity to truly love our self. In speaking of learning to love our truest self, Eckhart is not referring to egoism: he means our common human nature. This nature we share with all women and men, but especially with the God-Man Jesus Christ. The sail that catches only half the wind is a pastoral illustration, sensitive in its concession that most of us can't love this perfectly. Yet it stresses our capacity to learn to love our true self so as to love others. For some of us, this love might only extend to a friend. This is clearly a start; at least such a person is upon the Seas of Love.

III. (from Sermon 51)

Cracking the Shell

Sermon text: Exodus 20:12, which Eckhart translates as "You should honour father and mother."

Eckhart expands on this commandment so that it includes not only our parents but all who have spiritual power, those who bestow temporal goods, and our heavenly Father. Eckhart wants to illustrate how everything that bears a likeness to God, or a similitude, is in fact honouring God by this imitation. For our part, we need to look beyond the apparent in order to see this honouring at work.

I have said at times: The shell must be broken and what is within must come out. If you want to have the kernel, you must crack the shell. Consequently, if you want to discover naked [human] nature, you must in its similitude break open everything. Furthermore you [must] step therein [where] you are nearest to being-ness. So when you find the One where everything is One, stand there, one with the One. Who praises God? The divine praise standing in all things [praises God]. (DW 2:51.473–4)

Reflection

- How do you get to the true inner reality of who you are?
- What "shell" is keeping you from oneness?

Commentary

This is an apt illustration since so much of our lives can be spent centring on the shell. As good and valuable as many things can be to living the life of Christian perfection, we ultimately need to get to the meat of it all. Often in life this cracking of the shell is a long process, since first the pressures find resistance, then slowly fissures form and we finally realize that there is something within. This is also true of all of life, of all of creation. We really shouldn't presume that the shell is the nut; yet we do. So much of Eckhart's spirituality calls us to the essential ground of being, what is most within, where one is closest to the ground of being. "Standing out" (*ex-sistere*) from this essential ground is existence itself, and it is this "to be" which praises God in all of creation.

IV. (from Sermon 54b)

Divine Fusion

Sermon Text: John 17:3, which Eckhart translates as "This is eternal life, that they know you the one true God and Him whom you sent, Jesus Christ."

In this sermon, Eckhart is faced with explaining prayer and focuses on John 17:1, "He raised his eyes up from below," to demonstrate the importance of humility in prayer. Eckhart wants his listeners to realize how lowly things are able to receive something great.

All bodily creatures are a lure to the sun and stars, which effect [even] in stones their powers and likeness. When the sun draws to itself the moist air, when it gives to the stone its likeness and power, it imperceptibly allows for a fusion or power from within itself [to be given]. This power draws near to some metals, and some flesh and bones, and coming near to them must remain there. In such a way divine fusion takes place. God draws the soul and unites it with him and makes [the soul] Godly. [It is] as if one took a glass of water and placed it on top of a large vat of wine. [Being] right next to it the wine gives to the water the wine's powers, its nature and its colour. If it is red wine the water becomes red. If it is white wine the water turns white and becomes wine. This comes about due to its fusing

with the bouquet of the wine. What does this mean?
A very good question. [It means that] as by fusion the
wine breaks into the water, so too in every possible way
God breaks into the soul. Whoever wants to become
Godly should draw near with whole[-hearted] effort.
(DW 2:54b.567-68)

Reflection

- Does prayer have an impact on your life?
- What are the Godly things that you make an effort to
  be near? Make a list of them.

Commentary

This sermon gives us a glimpse into the interest of Eckhart's
day regarding the powers and properties of created materials.
Facts that we have forgotten, intrigued medieval chemists or
alchemists. St. Albert the Great, a Dominican who may have
taught Eckhart in Cologne, was a keen student of various
animals, plants and minerals. Alchemy was not the occult
science we may think of today; for the medieval thinker it
reflected a fundamental belief in the interconnectedness of
the cosmos. Just as there are seven planets, the (al)chemists
identified seven basic elements. It was common for spiritual
writers to speak of seven stages or steps in the life of Christian
perfection. Consequently, it makes perfect sense for Eckhart
to discuss the fact that certain stones and iron appropriate to
themselves the properties of other external objects – in this
case, the capacity that water has to absorb the taste and smell
of proximate objects. We may have observed this when a con-
tainer of drinking water in our refrigerator has been left open
alongside the leftover uncovered fish. This fact illustrates for
Eckhart's audience how the soul that is close to divine goodness
appropriates the properties of divine goodness. The closer we
are to Godly realities, the more God pours out divine life into
the soul, in a manner proper to our human nature.

V. (from Sermon 58)

Heaven on Sale

Sermon Text: John 12:26, which Eckhart translates as "Whoever serves me should follow me and where I am there my servant should be with me."

This sermon treats discipleship and the demands of following Christ into the non-material, into a spiritual letting go of the material things. In this illustration he wants to sell his audience on the value of letting go of material things, of being less materialistic.

One might notice how difficult it is for people who do not know spiritual things to let go of material things. As I have often said, "Why can't the ear taste sweet things the way the mouth does?" Because it is not suited to it. [So too] a fleshly person knows not spiritual things since he [or she] is not suited to them. Consequently it is possible for such an enlightened person to leave all materialistic things because [he or she] knows spiritual things. Saint Dionysius says, "God offers His heavenly kingdom for sale, and there is no [better] bargain than the heavenly kingdom since it is on sale." There is no possession, once purchased, that is as noble and as blessed. That's why he says it is a bargain since it sells for whatever each can afford. Therefore one should give everything that he [or she] possesses [in order to get] the kingdom of heaven, [namely] your own will. The will that is kept in self-will hasn't [really] purchased the heavenly kingdom. The one who lets go of self and of one's own will is free to let go of all material things. (DW 2:58.611–12)

Reflection

- What possessions possess you?
- What do you need to let go of?

Commentary

In an emerging materialistic society, namely mercantilism, Eckhart hawks heaven as a bargain. One can't help but be hooked by such a bargain. Mercantilism, materialism and, in our day, consumerism make us not only attached to things: our very selves become invested in them as well. Our wills become so attached to the power, prestige, status or importance of things that it is difficult to let go of material things when the immaterial or spiritual things are offered. Clearly, for Eckhart the volitional life of desire, of our selfish wants, can be converted to acquire what we think is impossible – namely, the heavenly kingdom – if only we give our will to God. Here the common Eckhartian theme of letting go surfaces as Eckhart tells his listeners to let go of the selfish will so we can receive the heavenly realm that is the spiritual in our own lives. It really is a bargain, because everyone has just the right amount to buy it: our will, given to God. In so doing, we acquire heaven and taste the spiritual in the midst of the material world.

VI. (from Sermon 59)

An Imperial Apple

Sermon Text: Daniel 3:41, which Eckhart translates as "We follow you with our entire heart; we fear you and seek your countenance."

This sermon addresses our attitude towards things and wisdom's demand to regard created things rightly. At this point in the sermon, Eckhart addresses the exhortation of Christ to "Deny yourself and pick up your cross" (Luke 9:23) not as a call to suffering, but as a call to see that such denial brings joy in its realization of the source of life. This illustration indicates why this gift is so important, in spite of its apparent commonness.

Many things which [we consider to be properly] rational are incidental, but life is proper to rational creatures as their essence [or being]. Therefore [God] says: "I give life" since one's being is one's life. God gives Himself completely when he says, "I give." No creature is capable of this giving, were it possible for a creature to give [it], God, who so caringly loves the soul, would not allow it, for He desires to give it Himself. Given by a creature the soul would find it of little value, as insignificant as a gnat. Just as if an emperor gave an apple to a person, [that person] would regard it more highly than if someone else gave him a [fine] cloak. So too the soul [would find it] insufferable if she had to receive [life] from anyone other than God. That is why He says, "I give," so the soul will have perfect joy in having been given [life]. (DW 2:59.630–31)

Reflection

- Who gives life?
- How precious is the gift of life?

Commentary

The holiness of human life is demonstrated in this passage. Human life finds its holiness in its source. Life, proper to rational creatures, is a gift from God. This reality is the basis for Eckhart's sense of the divine in creation. If we realize that life itself comes directly from God, we can see that the very *esse*, the "to be" or the "is-ing" of all things and of all humanity, is a gift and a participation in the divine. This is highly appropriate for our age, which has become a culture of death, treating life – through abortion and violence, poverty and euthanasia – as worthless. It is only in regarding the source of life that one comes to a proper appreciation of its worth. If we continue to consider life as nothing more than a primordial hiccup from some evolutionary stew or something biologically engineered, it becomes like a gnat. No wonder this modern age has seen so many atrocities, so many crimes against humanity. The apple, as with life, can be seen in itself as not much more than an apple, but when we reflect upon the giver of this gift, even if we think it insignificant in itself, it will take on incredible value due to its source. Regardless of the apple's markings, colour or taste, what gives it great worth is the emperor's having given it. So, too, with human life: regardless of a person's condition, sickness or health, wealth or poverty, the gift is so sacred because it is given directly by God.

VII. (from Sermon 59)

The Hound

Sermon Text: Daniel 3:41, as previously given.

As Eckhart ends this sermon on our whole-hearted following of Christ, he illustrates the importance of both perseverance and genuinely following after Christ.

A Master said: God's lowest is full of all creation and His highest is nowhere. I will tell you a story – [one day] someone asked a holy person what it meant that at times she relished contemplation and prayer while at other times she took no delight in anything. [The holy person] answered in this way: the hound which has spotted a rabbit follows the scent and is after the rabbit chasing its trail. But the other [hounds, not scenting, only] seeing the one running also enter the chase, but they tire out and give up. So it is with people who have seen God, caught the scent of God, they do not give up but always chase [after Him]. Therefore, David says, "Taste and see how sweet is the Lord" [Ps. 33.9/NRSV 34.8]. Such a person never grows weary but the others wear out. Some people run ahead of God, some [run] alongside of God and some follow after God. The ones running in front of God are those following their own will and not desiring to love the will of God, they are absolutely wrong. The others, who go alongside of God, say, "Lord, I desire nothing other than to do your will," [but] if they get sick they'd be glad if God's will were to make them well, so that [they] might endure. The third [group] follows after God, whatever He desires they follow Him willingly, and these are the perfect [ones]. Therefore St. John says in the Book of the Virtuous "They follow after the Lamb wherever He goes" [Rev.14.4]. These people follow after God no matter where He leads them, in sickness or in health, in good fortune or in misfortune. St. Peter ventured ahead of God and our Lord said, "Get behind me you Satan" [Matt. 16.23]. Now our Lord says, "I am in the Father, and the Father is in me" [John 14.11]. So it is that God is in the soul and your soul is in God. (DW 2:59.633-35)

Reflection

- How do you follow Christ?
- Have you caught God's scent or do you merely join the chase?

Commentary

This illustration begins by reminding the listener of God's immanent presence in creation, yet at the same time of God's absolute transcendence. Eckhart does this to help explain the spiritual aridity people experience. The person's question to Eckhart about endurance in living Christian perfection leads into the story of the hound. So often people look for God in ways they see other people looking for God, but never really catch the "scent of God." All of creation is full of God's presence, but we each must spot and seek it: as the Psalmist says, "Taste and see." However, we grow weary of prayer and contemplation if they don't keep us on the trail of our desired object. Rather than following Christ, we walk ahead or alongside or we completely give up. When illness or setbacks come, we want God to take them away. We must get on God's scent and follow that alone: follow God's will for us. In order to do this, we must, like the hound, catch sight of God and follow after God's scent; this takes place within the soul, where God is ever one.

VIII. (from Sermon 79)

God Makes Merry and Laughs

Sermon Text: Isaiah 49:13, which Eckhart translates as "Rejoice you heaven and earth, God has consoled his people and will forgive them all their sins."

This sermon treats God's desire for us to follow him in our caring for the needy, because God gives himself to the needy.

Now note the first passage spoken by the prophet, "Rejoice you heaven and earth." Truly, truly, by God, by God, and know this as you [know] God lives! At the least good longing all the saints in heaven and on earth rejoice. And all the angels rejoice with such joy, a joy that the world cannot come near to in the least. For each saint, the higher she is, the greater is her joy. And all their joy taken together is as small as a lentil compared to the joy God has in that deed. God makes merry and laughs in these good works, but all other works which do not reveal God's glory, these are considered like ash before God. Therefore he says: "Rejoice you heaven and earth, God has consoled his people." (DW 3:79.364-5)

Reflection

- When was the last time you said to yourself, "God is really pleased with me"?
- Why do we focus so much on what displeases God and not on what delights God?

Commentary

In this passage we see that Eckhart is no advocate of a spirituality that promotes escaping from the world. He is a contemplative who sees the active life as intimately linked to the delight of God. His focus is on our lives and not on God's reaction, since, properly speaking, God is beyond our control. Here we see that on our part, even the slightest inkling towards doing the good brings great joy to heaven and earth. And as great as that joy is, it is insignificant to the delight God takes in our goodness. It is such good works that bring God the greatest joy, laughter and merriment. All the other stupid things we do are like ash to God. But our good deeds bring delight.

We sense a kind of reverse psychology at work here. Rather than approaching our doing of good deeds from a penitential perspective, to make amends for our sins, Eckhart takes the opposite approach. We ought to do good deeds because they give God the greatest joy. It seems as though Eckhart is telling us that, in the end, these good deeds are the only ones that really matter. Anything else that we do or have done, God treats as so much dust in comparison to the good that we do. No wonder Eckhart is so excited at the start of this passage, underscoring its importance. It is as though he wants us to realize that our preoccupation with sins and misdeeds is not at all what God is interested in. Rather, God pays the most attention to the good that we make present. Truly, even our least good deeds, desires and longings bring joy to both heaven and earth. In these, God delights to the point of laughter.

IX. (from Sermon 81)

Virtues and an Anchor

Sermon Text: Psalm 45:5, which Eckhart translates as "The rapids, or the surging stream, have delighted the city of God."

This sermon treats the inner unity of the person while in the midst of various activities. It is a message well suited to our hectic world.

I have sometimes said, "A beginner in the goodly life should begin by holding on to this illustration." A person who wants to make a circle must first fix [the compass's] point, keeping it steady until the circle is drawn. In doing so, the circle will be well made. This is also true with people who must first learn to let their heart be steady, so that it will fix all of one's works. Regardless of the many things one does, if a person's heart is not fixed [the works] do him or her no good.

The Masters [at Paris] were of two opinions. One side held that nothing is able to move the good person, which they taught with many beautiful arguments. The other side [did not hold this, but held] that it is possible for a good person to be moved. And this [they held,] was found in the Sacred Scriptures. One can be moved and disturbed, but not overthrown. Our Lord Jesus Christ was often moved, as well as many other holy [women and men]. They were distraught, but never thrown from the virtuous [way]. They are like people who travel by water, when they want to sleep they cast the anchor into the water. They have found that this fixes the ship, while they float upon the water, but they are not carried away. I have said that the perfect person is unable to be easily hindered, but if little things distress one, he or she, is not in perfection. (DW 3:81.397–98)

Reflection

- What sorts of things disturb you?
- Do these things set you adrift?
- Can you be disturbed yet remain anchored?

Commentary

Eckhart is offering us a valuable lesson about the central point of spirituality. It is not to become so dispassionate that we are set like stone, unfeeling and uncaring. This is not how the saints and Christ were. Rather, we are to keep our still point in the midst of all kinds of adversity. There is a difference between being immovable and possessing the moral resolve that is rooted and not able to be deterred.

The image of the anchor reminds us all of a depth dimension that is necessary in the spiritual life. It enables us to remain in the river of life, with all that the passing currents and raging waves may bring. We thus remain firm in the virtuous life, even when we are distraught.

However, Eckhart cautions us, if we become distraught over every little thing that comes along, then there is something missing. We need to be anchored in a depth reality to live the virtuous life. This is especially worthwhile for people today who are engaged in active ministries. Something is missing if we are not deeply anchored in contemplation. If we are anchored in contemplation, we can endure adversity. An activist who is not anchored becomes distressed over little things and can easily slip from the virtuous side of justice to an unhealthy and destructive side of self-righteousness and condemnation.

X. (from Pfeiffer 75)

Fear Stitches Love

Sermon Text: John 16:7, 14:2. Evan's translation of Eckhart on this passage is "It is expedient for you, it is for your good, that I should go, for while I am with you the Holy Ghost the Comforter will not come to you."

According to the critical edition of Eckhart's sermons, this sermon, by its exclusion, is not considered authentically his. However, its themes are clearly those of Eckhart. Pfeiffer cites it as an Ascension Day sermon. The majority of the sermon is in fact on the consequences of the Ascension, inspired by John 14:2: "I will leave you, that I may prepare a place for you." This illustration appears early in the sermon and explains 1 John 4:18: "Love drives out fear."

> Our Lord will not suffer his lovers to be troubled, for fear is painful. And St. John says, "Love casteth out fear." Love is incompatible with fear and pain, for the waxing of love is the waning of fear, and when love is perfect all fear is gone. But at the beginning of the virtuous life fear is of use to man, providing him a thoroughfare for love. As the bodkin or the awl makes a passage for the thread and the shoe is stitched with thread, not with the iron; and as the bristle's part towards the thread is to put it in as fastening while the bristle is withdrawn; so, to begin with, fear makes room for love and love binds to God, whereas fear passes out. (Evans, 183)

Reflection

- What things do you fear?
- Do such fears open you up to something more, or do you try to avoid them?

Commentary

Here Eckhart explains the importance of fear in developing our moral life of virtue. Fear and love seem to be opposite to one another, and surely God does not desire his beloved to love out of fear. However much fear and pain are a necessary part of life, they are only a part. In living the life of virtue we begin fearing the loss of the beloved, and we dread the pains of judgment. This teaches us what love is all about and what a life of virtue, lived from love, means. Without this "stitching," our love and the strength of our virtues – our living – would depend on external things and would never be sewn to God.

156

6

Conclusion

The Christian mystics are a rich resource in the spiritual life. Their mysticism knows the mystery of God's incarnate presence in our world. They provide us with an abundant resource in the art of living, but this resource is not always easily accessible and requires us to break through to the ground of life. Too often we confuse the Christian mystics with esoteric and occult figures, thereby overlooking their great contributions to actually living the Christian life. They know something of God's revelation in Christ that warrants our study of their life and spirituality. In the case of someone like Eckhart, our challenge in reading him is complicated by the philosophical complexity of his ideas and his innovative language. How does one find the words to describe that which is beyond words? While I present an introduction to the person of Meister Eckhart, I have also sought to invite readers into his mystical thought, the mystery of God.

A conclusion, one would expect, ought to give the final word on the previous chapters, but with Eckhart, this is difficult to do. Is such a conclusion possible? I am aware that various books on Eckhart offer clear assertions, and the reader feels that he or she has obtained some handle on this mystic. If this is true, then Eckhart is a many-handled mug and all handles would be suitable for holding. However, I can't help but believe that while true, this might not be right. It seems to me that one can drink more fully of Eckhart if one grasps his concept of the soul, the handle of his anthropology, his sense of wherein lies our truest self.

It is his sense of the soul, what we today can rightly call his Christian anthropology, that holds the key to understanding Eckhart. Who we are as human beings – our purpose, our destiny, our meaning – is found in this sacred ground. His use of *exempla* in preaching provides a helpful tool by which even modern readers can catch the spiritual depth of his thought, for most of us lack the mental fitness required to jump right into Eckhart. This ought not to deter us from reading Eckhart, but it should tell us that our capacity to read and understand him will grow as our capacity for thought grows. Just as we can be out of shape physically, we can be out of shape mentally. No doubt some people will have set this book aside as too difficult in parts. Unfortunately, they stopped too soon. There are incredibly complex and difficult ideas in Eckhart that baffle even the most gifted reader. However, we need to exercise our intelligence so it will strengthen in order to engage the full force of Eckhart. To begin, the mind grows by using what is known, or familiar, such as the *exempla*, and develops its capacities from there. Such a development of the mind is at the heart of Eckhart's mysticism. Here is where we face the very meaning of life – body and soul, life and spirit are mysterious parts of this inner true self.

Human life is both outer and inner, material and spiritual. There is richness in our keeping the values of both of these aspects of life, especially at a time when we are so driven by the external life. Eckhart's point is an appropriate one, I think, especially given our modern pace of doing things. Most of us have forgotten the importance of a mature inner life, knowing and being the person we most truly are. Instead, we are confused by our compulsive addictions, not knowing our true self. This twofold reality of human existence, with its inner life and outer life, makes up the essential anthropology that is so crucial in all of Eckhart's thought. We saw this integration in Eckhart's *exempla* of the "two eyes" and others treated in Chapter 4. The concept of the soul is the key for pushing our own mind towards the kind of receptivity required if we are to both understand and experience Eckhart's mysticism. It is there, in the soul, with all of its facets, that the divine breaks into the human. The human must be readied to receive this presence and to live rooted in this Godly ground.

For the modern reader, the challenge of this soul concept and the kind of life it requires will seem mentally strenuous. We've grown comfortable with what is familiar to us, and our lives are too often mechanical. Compulsive behaviour prevents us from developing our receptivity to the Godly. I have encountered two kinds of readers when it comes to Eckhart: one superficial, and the other not. The second type of reader tries to stretch the mind, haunted by ideas that keep the mind working. The superficial reader gives up upon encountering the first struggle, whereas the committed reader keeps coming back, like an athlete with a goal, wanting to reach beyond the limits.

It was in Part III, with its series of *exempla*, that the reader ventured into the thought of Eckhart and began to discover the kind of mysticism this great thinker preached along with his spirituality. In these *exempla* we can see Eckhart's spirituality arising from the inner depth of the person. It is a spirituality practised in perfect love for all others. So often we do not look beyond the surface of things, but later find that in breaking beyond the outer crust or shell of things, we get to the divine presence. This presence acts upon us, transforming us, often in ways that we do not understand. But it requires of us nothing more than our will, which we are to give to God. What an incredible bargain, to see the world in this fashion. In having this kind of faith, we discover that even life itself is the most sacred gift because of the giver of the gift. Yes, Eckhart's spirituality is aware that sometimes we get off the track; we lose the scent of God. It is when we strive to sniff out the good that we give God great delight. For our part, we need to fix our hearts on God, and in this action, true virtue lies. Even in the midst of this virtuous striving, fear plays its role in binding us more closely to the love of God.

While they are simple illustrations, the *exempla* provide a start for most readers. They help us to grasp Eckhart's spirituality. While each reader might use different words to talk about Eckhart, these ten illustrations provide a core for each person to begin a basic reading of Eckhart. More important, they present some valuable tools for critically reading and assessing the many works on Eckhart. Other worthwhile works introduce the reader to the complex aspects of Eckhart's language and spirituality.

This work has had the modest task of using the preacher's *exempla* as a guide to some of the basic notions of his thought. His life, too, serves as a guide and helps us to read elements of his thought in light of the integrity of his life. Here is a man esteemed by his order, a Master of Paris, a popular preacher whose life ended in some unknown place, forgotten for centuries. Many people have no idea how trusted and respected he was as a member of his Dominican Order. No doubt his ideas continued in the writings of his Dominican students, such as Johannes Tauler and Heinrich Suso, great spiritual masters in their own right. But even with the respect of his brothers, he was long forgotten and thought to be one condemned. In the end, Eckhart trusted the truth of his life, for it was lived from a Godly ground; because of that we see the impact of his life and spirituality today. In 1992, the Dominican General Chapter in Mexico City accepted the findings of a special commission that determined that Eckhart and his essential teachings were in no need of a juridical "rehabilitation," the formal process of restoring him to good favour. The late Pope John Paul II had favourably quoted Eckhart in 1985, signalling his acceptability with no contrary action from the Vatican. Even in death he has been exonerated, albeit in an almost hidden way.

The more we study Eckhart, the more we discover a persistent truth. Eckhart's life is testimony to the impact all our lives have. Here we see how even a great life was reduced to the hidden recesses of history. Considered by some to be condemned, for centuries he was unknown and ignored. Yet even here the buried, hidden, denied aspects of life resurface. Like green shoots that break through barren ground, our inner self brings forth new levels of awareness, brings forth a new birth. After Eckhart's death the centuries hid him away. He emerged again in a century of world wars, a century desperate in its despair of God. Slowly the scent of this Godly man was tracked by scholars and modern-day mystics. The power of a forgotten medieval preacher once again speaks to the hunger of the human heart. In time, this restoration of his writings by scholars and the rehabilitation of his holiness by the Church testified to the Godly ground of his life. The ground of who we are is something Godly, and a life lived from that ground is a great life.

Appendix
Key Terms

Alois Haas, who is one of the great Eckhart scholars, identified four elements in Eckhart's program: purity of the divine nature, conformity to God, detachment, and the nobility of the soul.[1] The following appendix presents some of Eckhart's key terms according to four similarly fundamental themes: God's relation to us; our relation to God; our disposition in life; and our destiny in life. They provide helpful tools in understanding his theology.

Meister Eckhart's vocabulary is theologically rich and presents a challenge. This offers a special richness to Eckhart's mysticism, since his terminology[2] contributes a great deal to his spirituality. This thematic appendix is valuable because Eckhart uses Scholastic Latin and creatively employs Middle High German (MHG). Furthermore, modern German does not always do justice to the MHG concept, and English translations of the modern German can at times further complicate our efforts to understand his concepts. A thematic presentation helps us appreciate Eckhart's language in light of his spirituality without requiring us to study German and Latin.

1. God's relation to us

If we are to understand "God's relation to us," there needs to be a capacity within us as human beings for this action to happen in a way that does not diminish God's sovereignty or destroy our human nature. Eckhart's way of talking about this is found in three themes: Godly rootedness, divine nearness, and oneness.

Godly rootedness

A popular theme in Eckhart's preaching[3] is the relationship between God and the human soul. It is frequently understood

162

as *synderesis*, a philosophical word that conveys humankind's capacity for moral right judgment, or *scintilla animae*, which describes this as a spark of the divine in the soul.[4] In his preaching we find a number of related terms. He will use the image of place for this Godly rootedness, such as castle (*castellum*), temple (*templum*), town (*burgerlîn*), or the inner man (*innern menschen*). He also speaks of God's relation to us in the best of what is human, the noble (*daz edele*) or the highest (*oberste*). It is this spark (*vünkelîn*) of divinity, or God's grace, that allows us to be rooted in God.

Divine Nearness

God also relates to us in divine nearness or immanence. The terms particularly help us understand how God is the "presently present God." This presence is in no thing, and through no thing, not even in or through time. Eckhart's vocabulary speaks of it as our being stripped of what is not God: pureness (*lûterkeit*), emptiness (*ledickeit*), nakedness (*blôzheit*). He also conveys God's reverence in ideas of God's immediacy or "instantaneity," God's being without created mediation (*âne mittel*). This is also true of time in his sense of the now. Eckhart often speaks of it as the *eternal* now (*ewige nû*), this now (*disem nû*), this present now (*disem gegenwertigen nû*), the *eternal* now (*dem êwigen nû*), that now (*daz nû*), a present now (*einem gegenwertigen nû*), and an essential now (*einem wesenlîchen nû*).[5]

Oneness

The notion of oneness or unity is fundamental to Eckhart and is, ironically, quite complex. It suggests not only God's Absolute Oneness, but also the goal and end of that union seen in the inseparability of God and the soul. It is the oneness of the divine persons in the ground of divine being. This notion is found in his Latin and German works, using terms such as one (*unum/ein*), oneness (*unio/einicheit*), and simplicity (*simplicitas/einvalticheit*).

These three general notions – Godly rootedness, divine nearness, and oneness – are ways of appreciating that God is near to us, very near indeed.

2. Our relation to God

However, as created beings we are creatures, and our creatureliness is a reality. It is a theological obstacle in maintaining human integrity without diminishing divine sovereignty. Eckhart draws on a vocabulary of being (called ontology) to explain this problem. The sense of our human existence is the most immediate human experience of something divine; it is existence itself. This locates the person; it is from this that humankind gives birth to the divine. Eckhart's language falls into two major themes: beingness and groundedness.

Beingness

The mysterious wonder of existence itself is a source of Eckhart's mysticism and our relationship to God. He uses basic but very complex notions like essence (*wesen*); the is-ing of is-ness (*isticheit*), and the infinitive "to be" (*esse/sîn*). Existence – to be or not to be, to borrow from Shakespeare – is something of God being shared with us, our beingness itself.

Groundedness

Our existence is the most fundamentally undeniable aspect of who we are, and it is here that we find God. Eckhart speaks of this as ground (*grund*), or the noble ground (*edelsten grunde*), or the inmost ground (*innersten grunde*). But it is also where we are nearest to God, which he describes as the ground of the soul (*grunde der sêle*),[6] in the ground of divinity (*in dem grund der gothait*), and in the ground of divine essence (*in dem grunde götlîches wesens*).[7] The Latin notion of principle (*principium*) is akin to his concept of ground. In locating our self in our ground or principle, we are most open to relating to God, the Divine essence.[8]

164

3. Our disposition in life

Given the relationship that exists between the ground and its divine source, we are transformed in a way that transforms our world. Transforming our world means that there must be a moral or ethical dimension to life. Eckhart's spirituality maintains a balance between the inner ground where we relate to God, and at the same time, our relating to the world in which we live without becoming lost in that world. He presents this in the themes of "unattachedness" and "ownerlessness." They are how Eckhart speaks about one's disposition in life.

Unattachedness

This concept of being unattached is confusing, especially when we translate it as detachment. One can be unattached to things and still acknowledge their reality. Detachment, on the other hand, too often implies a complete rejection of the thing. This is an important distinction when we think of our relationship to the world. For Eckhart, we realize what the world is, and we are not detached from the demands of living in the world. The terms used are letting-go-ness (*gelâzenheit*) with its root form to let go (*lâzen*), as well as the similar term cut-loose-ness (*abegescheidenheit*), which is better translated as unattachment.

Ownerlessness

Another aspect of our disposition in the world is to realize that we do not own anything. It is an attitude in life that sees everything as somehow on loan from God. His vocabulary for this notion includes "without ownership" (*âne eigenschaft*) when it comes to things, and as "without why" (*âne war umbe*) when it comes to intellectual things. In Latin this concept is seen as property (*proprietas*). The reason for such a disposition is to foster a pure spirit (*ledic gemüete*), free to do God's will.

Both notions are meant to free us for life in this world that is given to God. We cannot see the world as evil in itself; at the same time, we know that we are not limited to the realities of this world. There is something more; in a certain sense, this world is just its wrappings: good and beautiful, but not the real gift.

4. Our destiny in life

The difficult task for Eckhart is addressing how the mystery of created human existence "manifests" or "incarnates" the divine nearness. This is, for Eckhart, the goal of human existence, and needs to modestly not overextend the claims humanity has on salvation, while allowing for salvation to be something that can be realized by grace.

Image

Eckhart's mystical language employs the notion of "image" (*bilde*) as something of our sense of sight and the soul's mysterious ability to retain an image even when it is not present. The image of a friend painted on the wall and that image in our mind disclose something of our image in Christ. Ultimately, we are destined for this divine image, provided we truly are its image.

Birthing God

Another concept that Eckhart employs for this sense of destiny is that of birthing, or "birthing God" (*Gottesgeburt*). This is our destiny, both in this life and in the life to come. In this world we are called to bring forth, to manifest an aspect of the Incarnation. In our ultimate destiny we are born into the Mystical Body of Christ.

Image and Divine Birthing are ways that Eckhart talks about the complex mystery of our destiny. They are concepts that require thought and reflection, for there is something incarnational in both.

Notes

Introduction

1   Vita erat lux hominum, moraliter vul dicere quod vita aedificat et illuminat proximum plus quam verba. *Expositio sancti Evangelii secundum Iohannem*, 3:69.57 (LW). *Meister Eckhart: Die deutschen und lateinischen Werke. Herausgegeben im Auftrage der Deutschen Forschungsgemeinschaft.* Stuttgart and Berlin: Verlag W. Kohlhammer, 11 Vols., 1936–. (Hereafter DW for the *Deutschen Werke* and LW for the *Lateinischen Werke*).

2   *Master Eckhart: Parisian Questions and Prologues*, Armand Maurer, ed. (Toronto: Pontifical Institute Medieval Studies, 1974), 59. This text is actually found in Gonsalvo's response and is a summation of Eckhart's position: Item: ipsum intelligere quaedem deiformitas vel deiformatio, quia ipse deus est ipsum intelligere et non est esse (*Quaestiones Parisienses* III, LW IV n.9, p.60).

3   Nostra enim operatio sicut et scientia a rebus oritur; propter quod a rebus dependet et mutatur rebus mutatis. E converso res ipsae ortum habent a scientia dei et dependent, propter quod ipsis, utpote posterioribus, mutatis deus in sua scientia non mutatus (*Expositio libri Genesis* LW I n.8, p.192).

4   This notion of relational knowing or ethical knowing is one Eckhart shares with Aquinas. For an explanation of this concept, see my article, "On the Persistence of Aquinas" in *Listening: Journal of Religion and Culture* 38 (2003):263–275.

5   Two works by Herman Schwarz promoted what has been called Rassenphilosophie (Race philosophy). They were: *Eckhart der Deutsche Völkische Religion im Aufgang* (Berlin: Junker und Dünnhaupt, 1935) and *Christentum, Nationalsozialismus und deutsche Glaubensbewegung* (Berlin: Junker und Dünnhaupt, 1938).

6   "Maître Eckhart: son programme spirituel de prédication," *La Vie spirituelle*, March 2002 (156):855–872, which is a translation by Uta Korzeniewski of Haas's 1984 article "Meister Eckharts geistliches Predigtprogramm," *Geistliches Mittelalter* (189–209).

7   Humbert of Romans (1200–1277) was elected Master in 1254. See "Humbert of Romans' Treatise on the Formation of Preachers" in *Early Dominicans Selected Writings*, Simon Tugwell, ed. (New York: Paulist Press, 1982), 183–370.

8   An excellent online source for these works can be found at the Web Gallery of Art (http://www.wga.hu).

9   An excellent work is *Medieval Texts and Images: Studies of Manuscripts from the Middle Ages*, eds. Margaret M. Manion & Bernard J. Muir (Chur, Switzerland: Harwood Academic Publishers, 1991).

Part I
Chapter 1

[1]   Georg Hofmann, *Johannes Tauler, Predigten I Vollständige Ausgabe* (Einsiedeln: Johannes Verlag, 1979), 103, cited in *Johannes Tauler, Sermons,* Maria Shrady, trans. (New York: Paulist Press, 1985), 28.

[2]   Taken from Eckhart's September 26th, 1326 declaration to the Cologne Tribunal.

[3]   Josef Koch, "Kritische Studien Zum Leben Meister Eckharts" II Parts *Achivum Fratrum Praedicatorum* 29(1959) and 30(1960), Pt. I, 5–51; Kurt Ruh, *Meister Eckhart: Theologe, Prediger, Mystiker* (München: Verlag C.H.Beck, 1985).

[4]   ...um 1277 ist Eckhart Student der Artes in Paris, vor 1280 beginnt er das Studium der Theologie in Köln, 1293/94 liest er die Sentenzen in Paris... (Josef Koch, Pt. I, 12).

[5]   Cf. Alain de Libera, *Introduction à la Mystique Rhenane d'Albert le Grand à Maître Eckhart* (Paris: O.E.I.L., 1984), 163.

[6]   Koch, Pt. I, 16.

[7]   Cf. *Monumenta ordinis Fratrum Praedicatorum Historica, III: Acta Capitulorum Generalium* vol I Benedict Maria Reichert, ed. (Rome: Sacred Congregation Propagation of Faith, 1898), 298.

[8]   ...Meißen, Thüringen, Hessen, Sachsen, Mark Brandenburg, Sclavonia (von Hamburg bis Stralsund reichend), Friesland, Westfalen, Seeland und Holland (Koch, Pt. I, 18).

[9]   Genoa (1305); Paris (1306); Padua (1308); and Saragossa (1309). Cf. *Acta Capitulorum Generalium* op.cit. v.2, 1–50.

[10] Während Eckharts Amtszeit, die im wesentlichen mit dem Generalat Aymerichs von Piacenza zusammemfällt, wurden drei Generalkapitel der Provinziale gehalten, und zwar in Toulouse (1304), Straßburg (1307) und Piacenza (1310). Er nahm an allen drei teil (Koch, Pt. I, 21).

[11] English Translation (hereafter ET): *Meister Eckhart, The Essential Sermons, Commentaries, Treatises and Defense,* trans. and ed. by Bernard McGinn and Edmund Colledge (New York: Paulist Press, 1981) 255 [hereafter *Essential.* Where appropriate I will indicate McGinn or Colledge as the source]. Der Mensch soll auch nie ein Werk so gut beurteilen noch als so recht ausführen, daß er je so frei oder so selbstsicher in den Werken werde, daß seine Vernunft je müßig werde oder einschlafe. Er soll sich ständig mit den beiden kräften der Vernunft und des Willens erheben und darin sein Allerbestes im höchsten Grade ergreifen und sich äußerlich und innerlich gegen jeden Schaden besonnen vorsehen; dann versäumt er nie etwas in irgendwelchen Dingen, sondern er nimmt ohne Unterlaß in hohem Grade zu (Reden der Unterweisung DW V, 512).

12   *Acta Capitulorum Generalium*, v.2, 53.

13   Koch, Pt. I, 30–33.

14   Koch, Pt. I, 35.

15   Die Geschichte der Gründing des Konventes in der freien Reichsstadt Dortmund (damals im Erzbistum Köln) ist eines der turbulentesten Kapitel in der Geschichte der deutschen Dominikaner (Koch, Pt. I, 33). Kurt Ruh incorrectly attributes this "turbulent" description of Koch's to the Dominican convent in Braunschweig (Ruh, 26).

16   Koch, Pt. I, 33–35 (I summarize).

17   Koch, Pt. I, 24–25.

18   Schließlich obsiegten sie aber, dank der tatkräftigen Unterstützung durch Papst Johannes XXII, und konnten am 24. März 1330 zu zwanzig sich endgültig niederlassen. (Quoted by Koch from J. Hansen in *Die Chroniken der dt. Städte*, vol. 20, p. 204. Koch, Pt. I, 34–5).

19   *Master Eckhart: Parisian Questions and Prologues.* Armand A. Maurer, CSB, trans. (Toronto: Pontifical Institute of Medieval Studies, 1974).

20   Koch, Pt. I, 17–18.

21   See "Explanatory Shards of the Incarnation in Eckhart's Parisian Questions." op. cit.

22   Ibid., 12.

23   Koch, Pt. I, 38–49.

24   Francis Rapp, "Le public de maître Eckhart à Strasbourg," *La Vie spirituelle* March 2002 156:873–885.

25   Ibid., 876.

26   Ibid., 878.

27   Ibid., 882.

Chapter 2

1   *Meister Eckhart, Sermons and Treatises*, M. O'C. Walshe, trans. and ed., vol. 1 (London & Dulverton: Element Books, 1979) xxvi.

2   Robert E. Lerner, *The Heresy of the Free Spirit in the Later Middle Ages* (Berkeley: University of California Press, 1972) p. 66 [Lerner cites *Concilia Germaniae*, J. Hartzheim, ed. (Cologne, 1759–90), IV, 100-102].

3   Ibid., 30.

4   R.W. Southern, "Western Society and the Church in the Middle Ages," Owen Chadwick. ed. *The Pelican History of the Church*, VI vols. (Middlesex, UK: Penguin, 1978), Vol. II, 325.

[5]   Lerner, 234–35.

[6]   Oliver Davies has put forward the theory that the reason for Eckhart's condemnation was due to just such a power brokering between John XXII and Henry of Virneburg. Cf. "Why were Eckhart's propositions condemned?" *New Blackfriars* (October 1990) 71:433–445.

[7]   Lerner, 236.

[8]   Koch, Pt. II, 22–26.

[9]   ...da Nikolaus noch 1327 Lektor war,... als Lektor unterstand Nikolaus dem Magister Eckhart, als Vikar des Generals und Visitator der Teutonia stand er über ihm und hatte die Aufgabe, dessen Lehre auf ihre Rechtgläubigkeit zu prüfen! Er war ja neben Eckhart der einzige theologische Fachmann am Kölner Generalstudium. Es ist unter diesen Umständen weder verwunderlich, da Nikolaus die Rechtgläubigkeit seines Magisters verteidigte, noch da die Kommissare des Erzbischofs dieser Verteidigung skeptisch gegenüberstanden (Koch, Pt. II, 14).

[10]   Ibid., Pt. II, 35–6.

[11]   Jeanne Ancelet-Hustache, *Master Eckhart and the Rhineland Mystics* (New York: Harper Torchbooks, 1957); Alois Dempf, *Meister Eckhart* (Freiburg: Herder, 1960); and Joseph Koch, "Kritische Studien zum Leben Meister Eckhart" art. cit. (1959/1960).

[12]   Bernard McGinn, "Eckhart's Condemnation Reconsidered," *The Thomist* 44 (1980), 391.

[13]   Ibid., 394.

[14]   Ibid., 395.

[15]   ET: *Essential* (McGinn), 71–72. LT: Ego frater Ekardus ordinis predicatorum prefatus respondeo. Primo protestor contra vobis commissariis magistro Renhera frisone, doctore theologie, et fratre Petro de Estate nuper custode ordinis fratrum minorum, quod juxta libertatem et privilegia ordinis nostri, coram vobis non teneor conparere nec objectis respondere, presertim cum non sim de heresi notatus aut unquam fuerim infamatus, teste omni vita mea et doctrina, acclamante opinione fratrum totius ordinis et populi utriusque sexus totius regni omnis rationis. Ex quo patet secundo quod commissio vobis facta a venerabili patre domino Coloniensi archiepiscopo, cujus vitam deus conservet, nullius est vigoris, utpote ex falsi suggestione, radice et arbore mala procedens Quinymo si minoris essem fame in populo et minoris zeli justitie certus sum quod contra me non essent talia ab emulis attemptata. Patienter tamen michi ferendum est quia beati qui patiuntur propter justitiam et deus flagellat omnem filium quem recipit secundum Apostolum, ut merito dicam cum psalmo: ego autem in flagella paratus sum, maxime cum jam pridem magistri theologie Parisius nostris temporibus mandatum habuerint superioris de examinandis libris preclarissimorum virorum sancti Thome de Aquino et

domini fratris Alberti, tanquam suspectis et erroneis. Et contra ipsum sanctum Thomam frequentur a multis scriptum est dictum et publice predicatum, quod errores et hereses scripserit et docuerit. Sed favente domino tam Parisius quam per ipsum summum pontificem et romanam curiam ipsius vita et doctrina pariter sunt approbata [Gabriel Théry, "Édition critique des pièces relatives au procès d'Eckhart contenues dans le manuscript 33b de la Bibliothèque de Soest," Archives d'histoire littéraire et doctrinale du moyen âge 1–2 (1926), 185].

16   McGinn, 394. Cf. Gabriel Théry, "Édition critique des pièces relatives au procès d'Eckhart contenues dans le manuscript 33b de la Bibliothèque de Soest," Archives d'histoire littéraire et doctrinale du moyen âge 1 (1926), 129-268.

17   ...utpote ex falsi suggestione, radice et arbore mala procedens Quinymo si minoris essem fame in populo et minoris zeli justitie... (Théry, 185).

18   *Essential* (Colledge), 294. Cf. DW V 432–4; 546–7. MHD: Dâ von ist abegescheidenheit daz aller beste, wan si reiniget die sêle und liutert die gewizzene und enzündet daz herze und wecket den geist und machet snel die begirde und tuot got erkennen und scheidet abe die crêatûre und vereiniget sich mit gote. Nû merket, alle vernünftigen menschen! Daz snelleste tier, daz iuch treget ze dirre volkomenheit, daz ist lîden, wan ez niuzet nieman mê êwiger süezicheit, dan die mit Kristô stânt in der groesten bitterkeit. Ez enist niht gelligers dan lîden und enist niht honicsamers dan geliten-hân; ez entstellet den lîp nihtes mêr vor den liuten dan lîden und enzieret aber die sêle vor gote nihtes mêr dan geliten-hân. Daz vesteste fundament, dar ûf disiu volkomenheit gestân mac, daz ist dêmüeticheit, wan swelhes natûre hie kriuchet in der tiefsten nider keit, des geist vliuget ûf in daz hoehste der gotheit, wan liebe bringet leit, und leit bringet liebe. Und dâ von, swer begert ze kommene ze volkomener abegescheidenheit, der stelle nâch volkomener demüeticheit, sô kumet er in die naehede der gotheit (DW V, 432–34).

19   Er beteuert seinen Abscheu gegen alle Irrlehren und alle sittlichen Verirrungen, erklärt sich bereit, alles von ihm Geschriebene, Gesagte oder Gepredigte zu widerrufen, sofern man nachweise, da es mit der gesunden kirchlichen Lehre unvereinbar sei, und nimmt zu drei Punkten, hinsichtlich derer er mi verstanden worden sei, besonders Stellung (Koch, Pt. II, 38–39). Cf. Laurent, 344–46.

20   Es ist eine Flucht in die Öffentlichkeit, die nach keiner Richtung eine günstige Wirkung haben konnte (Koch, Pt. II, 39).

21   Koch, Pt. II, 38.

22   Über den Ausgang des Prozesses gegen Eckhart herrschte in diesem Kreis in Frühsommer 1327 offensichlich eine optimistische Meinung, wie sich aus der Bemerkung ergibt, da niemand, der Meister Eckhart's Leben kenne, an dessen Glauben und heiligen Lebenswandel zweifeln dürfe (Koch, Pt. II, 40).

23   McGinn, 397.

24   The *Dictionnaire de Théologie catholique* article by F. Vernet suggests Eckhart died
      in 1327 based upon a work thus far unavailable to this researcher by W.Praeger
      (*Geschichte der deutschen Mystik*, vol. I, 362). Cf. F. Vernet *Dictionnaire de Théologic
      catholique* (Vacant-Mangenot) v. IV (Paris, 1920) col. 2059–2060.

25   Of the 28 articles, Eckhart acknowledged only 26 as his own. The bull divides
      these according to articles containing heresy (1–15, as well as the two rejected
      by Eckhart), and articles only suspected of heresy (16–26).

26   ET: *Essential* (McGinn), 80-81. LT: Porro, tam illis, apud quos prefati articuli
      predicati seu dogmatizati fuerunt, quam quibuslibet aliis ad quorum devenere
      notitiam volumus notum esse, quod, prout constat per publicum instrumentum
      inde confectum, prefatus Ekardus in fine vite sue fidem catholicam profitens
      predictos viginti sex articulos, quos se predicasse confessus extilit, necnon
      quecunque alia per eum scripta et docta, sive in scolis sive in predicationibus,
      que possent generare in mentibus fidelium sensum hereticum vel erroneum ae
      vere fidei inimicum, quantum ad illum sensum revocavit ac etiam reprobavit
      et haberi voluit pro simpliciter et totaliter revocatis, ac si illos et illa singil-
      latim et singulariter revocasset, determinationi apostolice sedis et nostre tam
      se quam scripta sua et dicta omnia summittendo [M-H Laurent "Autour du
      procès de Maitre Eckhart. Les documents des Archives Vaticanes," Divus
      Thomas (Piacenza) ser.III, 13 (1936) 444].

27   *Essential* (Colledge), 15.

28   Cf. Laurent, 446–47.

29   Cf. Laurent, 444–45. Quocirca fraternitati tue per apostolica scripta manda-
      mus, quatenus tenorem predictum, postquam eum diligenter inspexeris, per
      te vel per alium seu alios in tuis civitate, diocesi et provincia publices et facias
      solemniter publicari, ut per publicationem huiusmodi simplicium corda, qui
      faciliter seducunter, et maxime ille, quibus idem Ekardus, dum vixit, predictos
      articulos predicavit, erroribus contentis in eis minime imbuantur (445).

Part II
Chapter 3

1   *Summa Theologia* II II 23, 2.

2   Thomas Merton, *New Seeds of Contemplation* (New York: New Directions,
     1972).

3   See M. Demkovich "Explanatory Shards of the Incarnation in Eckhart's Parisian
     Questions" in the *Eckhart Review* (Spring 2004) 13: 5-24.

4   The standard adopted to indicate Eckhart's sermons is by using the numbers
     given them in the Kohlhamer critical edition, DW already cited above.

5   In Eckhart's day, biblical citations were a bit different from today, as he lived
     before the King James Bible and the modern critical editions of the Bible. If

you look for the text he mentions, you will find it is now verse 14:3, and is translated in the New Revised Standard Version of the Bible (hereafter NRSV) as "In you the orphan finds mercy."

6   *De Genesi ad Litteram vi*, ch 29, n.40 (PL 34,356).

7   DW 3, Pr. 61, 35-47.

Chapter 4

1   Cf. Michael Demkovich, "Beyond Subjectivity: Opening the Ego," *Listening: Journal of Religion and Culture* 29(1994):162–173.

2   The *New York Times* writer George Johnson takes on a modern overview of this struggle between science and faith in his work *Fire in the Mind: Science, Faith, and the Search for Order* (New York: Vintage Books, 1995).

3   See Hans Hof's *Scintilla Animae: Eine studie zu einem Grundbegriffe in Meister Eckharts Philosophie mit besonder Berücksichtigung des Verhaltnis der Eckhartischen Philosophie zur neoplatonischen und tomistischen Anschauung* (Lund: 1952).

4   A number of sermons not included in the Kohlhammer critical edition appeared in a collection of Eckhart's sermons published by Franz Pfeiffer (Leipzig: 1857). The text given here is from the translation of the Pfeiffer sermon 61 into English by C. de B. Evans, John M. Watkins publisher, London, 1947 (page 154).

Part III
Chapter 5

1   I use "fusion" in my translation of the Middle High German *brâdem*, which makes better sense given the alchemy overtone. The modern equivalents (*braten* in German and *braden* in Dutch) both mean to broil or roast. In the context of this sermon, it is more akin to the Latin *fusio*, the outpouring, or fusion. This is not unusual language for the times, since Albert the Great had already written on the fusion of iron in Book IV of *De mineralibus*.

Appendix

1   "Maître Eckhart: son programme spirituel de prédication," *La Vie spirituelle*. March 2002 (156:855-872), which is a translation by Uta Korzeniewski of Haas's 1984 article "Meister Eckharts geistliches Predigtprogramm," *Geistliches Mittelalter* (189–209).

2   Helpful works on Eckhart's vocabulary are Benno Schmoldt's *Die deutsche Begriffssprache Meister Eckharts: Studien zur philosophischen Terminologie des Mittelhochdeutschen* (Heidelberg: Quelle & Mayer, 1954); and Udo Nix' *Der mystische Wortschatz Meister Eckharts im Lichte der energetischen Sprachbetrachtung in Sprache und*

Gemeinschaft: Im Auftrag eines Arbeitskreises für deutsche Sprache. Leo Weisgerber. ed. (Düsseldorf: Pädagogischer Verlag Schwann, 1963).

[3]   Cf. pr. 2, 9, 17, 20a, 20b, 37, 38, 42, 48, 65, 76 and *Daz buouch der gotlîchen troestung* (DW V, 31–2) for appearances of *vunke* and *vünkelîn*.

[4]   Michel Tardieu "Psychaios Spinther: Histoire d'une métaphore dans la tradition platonicienne jusqu'à Eckhart," *Revue des Études Augustiniennes* 21 (1975):223–55.

[5]   *disem nû* (DW I pr.1, p.12,2); disem gegenwertigen nû (DW I pr.2, p.26,1); dem *êwigen nû* (DW I pr.2, p.34,2); *daz nû* (DW I pr.2, p.34,3); *einem gegenwertigen nû* (DW I pr.10, p.166,5); and *einem wesenlîchen nû* (DW I pr.10, p.166,9).

[6]   Cf. DW I pr. 2, p.31,2; pr. 5b, p. 87,6; and pr. 10, p.162,5.

[7]   Cf. DW I pr. 15, p.247,3 and pr. 24, p.419,4.

[8]   This is seen in sermon 5b: "Hereon spoke the brief text that I have put forth: 'God has sent his only begotten Son into the world.' This should not be understood of the outward world, as when he ate and drank with us, but it should be understood of the inner world. As truly as the Father in his simple nature begets his son naturally, so truly does he beget him in the inmost spirit, and this is the inner world. Here God's ground is my ground and my ground, God's ground." [Her umbe sprichet daz wörtlîn, daz ich vür geleit hân: 'got hât gesant sînen einbornen sun in die werlt'; daz sult ir niht verstân vür die ûzwendige werlt, als er mit uns az und trank: ir sult ez verstân vür die inner werlt. Als waerliche der vater in sîner einvaltigen natûre gebirt sînen sun natiurlîche, als gewaerlîche gebirt er i in des geistes innigestez, und diz ist diu inner werlt. Hie ist gotes grunt mîn grunt und mîn grunt gotes grunt (DW I pr 5b, p. 90).]

Bibliography

Sources

Augustine Daniels, O.S.B., ed. "Eine lateinische Rechtfertigungsschrift des Meister Eckharts." *Beiträge zur Geschichte der Philosophie des Mittelalters*, 23, 5 (Münster: Aschendorff, 1923): 1–4, 12–13, 34–35, 65–66.

Meister Eckhart: *Die deutschen und lateinischen Werke*. Herausgegeben im Auftrage der Deutschen Forschungsgemeinschaft. Stuttgart and Berlin: Verlag W. Kohlhammer, 11 Vols., 1936–.

Franz Jostes, ed. *Meister Eckhart und seine Jünger: Ungedruckte zur Geschichte der deutschen Mystik*. De Gruyter, 1972 (Series: *Deutsche Neudrucke Texte des Mittelalters*).

Thomas Kaepelli, O.P. "Kurz Mitteilungen über mittelalterliche Dominikanerschriftsteller." *Archivum Fratrum Praedicatorum* 10, (1940):293–94.

———. *Scriptores ordinis Praedicatorum medii aevi*. Vol. I (A-F). Rome, 1970.

Josef Koch. "Kritische Studien Zum Leben Meister Eckharts" II Parts *Achivum Fratrum Praedicatorum* 29 (1959):1–51 and 30 (1960):5–52.

M.H. Laurent. "Autour du procés de Maître Eckhart. Les documents des Archives Vaticanes." *Divus Thomas* (Piacenza) 39 (1936):331–48, 430–47.

Udo Nix. *Der mystische Wortschatz Meister Eckharts im Lichte der energetischen Sprachbetrachtung in Sprache und Gemeinschaft: Im Auftrag eines Arbeitskreises für deutsche Sprache*. Leo Weisgerber, ed. (Düsseldorf: Pädagogischer Verlag Schwann, 1963).

Josef Quint, ed. and trans. *Meister Eckehart: Deutsche Predigten und Traktate*. Munich: Carl Hanser, 1955.

Josef Quint, ed. *Textbuch zur Mystik des deutschen Mittelalters: Meister Eckhart, Johannes Tauler, Heinrich Seuse*. Halle/Saale: M. Niemeyer, 1952.

Benno Schmoldt. *Die deutsche Begriffssprache Meister Eckharts: Studien zur philosophischen Terminologie des Mittelhochdeutschen*. Heidelberg: Quelle & Mayer, 1954.

Gabriel Théry, O.P. "Édition critique des piéces relatives au procés d'Eckhart continues dans le manuscrit 33b de la Bibliotheque de Soest." *Archives d'histoire littéraire et doctrinal du moyen-âge*, 1 (1926):129–268.

Translations and commentaries

Meister Eckhart: A Modern Translation. Raymond B. Blakney, trans. New York: Harper Torchbooks, 1941.

James M. Clark. *Meister Eckhart: An Introduction to the Study of His Works with an Anthology of His Sermons*. Edinburgh: Thomas Nelson, 1957.

Treatises and Sermons of Meister Eckhart. James M. Clark and John V. Skinner, eds. and trans. New York: Octagon Books, 1983. (Reprint of Harper and Row ed., 1958.)

Meister Eckhart: Selected Writings, Oliver Davies, ed. and trans. London: Penguin, 1994.

C. de B. Evans. *Meister Eckhart by Franz Pfeiffer*. 2 vols. London: Watkins, 1924 and 1931.

Master Eckhart: Parisian Questions and Prologues. Armand Maurer, ed. and trans. Toronto: Pontifical Institute of Medieval Studies, 1974.

Meister Eckhart: The Essential Sermons, Commentaries, Treatises and Defense, trans. and ed. by Bernard McGinn and Edmund Colledge. New York: Paulist Press, 1981.

Meister Eckhart: Teacher and Preacher. Bernard McGinn and Frank Tobin, eds. and trans. New York and London: Paulist Press / SPCK, 1987.

Meister Eckhart: Sermons and Treatises, by M. O'C. Walshe, trans. 3 vols. Longmead, Shaftesbury, Dorset: Element Books, 1987.

Reiner Schürmann. *Meister Eckhart: Mystic and Philosopher*. Bloomington: Indiana University Press, 1978.

Secondary sources

Jeanne Ancelet-Hustache. *Master Eckhart and the Rhineland Mystics*. New York and London: Harper and Row / Longmans, 1957.

James M. Clark. *The Great German Mystics*. New York: Russell and Russell, 1970. (Reprint of Basil Blackwell edition, Oxford: 1949.)

Oliver Davies. *God Within: The Mystical Tradition of Northern Europe*. London: Darton, Longman and Todd, 1988.

————. "Why were Eckhart's propositions condemned?" *New Blackfriars* (October 1990) 71:433-445.

————. *Meister Eckhart: Mystical Theologian*. London: SPCK, 1991.

Alain de Libera. *Introduction a la Mystique Rhenane d'Albert le Grand à Maître Eckhart*. Paris: O.E.I.L., 1984.

Michael Demkovich. "On the Persistence of Aquinas," *Listening: Journal of Religion and Culture* 38 (2003):263–275.

————. "Explanatory Shards of the Incarnation in Eckhart's Parisian Questions." *Eckhart Review* (Spring 2004):13:5–24.

Alois Dempf. *Meister Eckhart*. Freiburg: Herder, 1960.

Robert K. Forman. *Meister Eckhart: Mystic as Theologian*. Rockport, MA: Element Books, 1991.

Alois Haas. "Maître Eckhart: son programme spirituel de prédication. " *La Vie spirituelle*. March 2002 156:855–872.

Amy Hollywood. *The Soul as Virgin Wife: Mechthild of Magdeburg, Marguerite Porete, and Meister Eckhart*. Notre Dame, IN: University of Notre Dame Press, 1996.

"Humbert of Romans' Treatise on the Formation of Preachers" in *Early Dominicans Selected Writings*. Simon Tugwell, ed. New York: Paulist Press, 1982, 183–370.

Rufus Jones. *The Flowering of Mysticism in the Fourteenth Century*. New York: Hafner Publishing Co., 1971 (facsimile of 1939 edition).

C.F. Kelly. *Meister Eckhart on Divine Knowledge*. New Haven and London: Yale University Press, 1977.

Robert E. Lerner. *The Heresy of the Free Spirit in the Later Middle Ages*. Berkeley: University of California Press, 1972.

Bernard McGinn. *The Mystical Thought of Meister Eckhart: The Man from Whom God Hid Nothing*, New York: Crossroads Publishing Co., 2001.

——. ed. *Meister Eckhart and the Beguine Mystics Hadewijch of Brabant, Mechthild of Magdeburg, and Marguerite Porete*. New York: Continuum, 1994.

——. "Eckhart's Condemnation Reconsidered." *The Thomist* 44 (1980): 390–414.

Francis Rapp. "Le public de maître Eckhart à Strasbourg." *La Vie spirituelle.* March 2002 156:873–885.

Wayne Simsic. *Praying with Meister Eckhart.* Winona, MN: Saint Mary's Press, 1998.

Cyprian Smith. *The Way of Paradox: Spiritual Life as Taught by Meister Eckhart.* New York: Paulist Press, 1988.

R.W. Southern. *Western Society and the Church in the Middle Ages.* Owen Chadwick, ed. *The Pelican History of the Church*, VI vols. Middlesex, UK: Penguin, 1978.

Michel Tardieu. "Psychaios Spinther: Histoire d'une métaphore dans la tradition platonicienne jusqu'à Eckhart." *Revue des Études Augustiniennes* 21 (1975):223–55.

Frank Tobin. *Meister Eckhart: Thought and Language.* Philadelphia: University of Pennsylvania Press, 1986.

Winfried Trusen. *Der Prozess gegen Meister Eckhart.* Fribourg: University of Fribourg, 1988.

Shizuteru Ueda. *Die Gottesgeburt in der Seele und der Durchbruch zur Gottheit. Die mystische Anthropologie Meister Eckharts und ihre Konfrontation mit der Mystik des Zen –Buddhismus.* Gütersloh: Mohn, 1965.

Andrew Weeks. *German Mysticism from Hildegard of Bingen to Ludwig Wittgenstein: A Literary and Intellectual History.* Albany, NY: State University of New York Press, 1993.

Richard Woods, O.P. *Eckhart's Way.* Wilmington, DE: Glazier, 1986 / Collegeville, MN: Liturgical Press, 1991.

——. "The Condemnation of Meister Eckhart." *Spirituality*, 33, 6 (Nov.–Dec. 2000):342–47.